the
POSITIVE SIDE
of the
STREET

Other Books by Napoleon Hill

Think and Grow Rich

Outwitting the Devil

Success Through a Positive Mental Attitude

The Law of Success

The Master to Key Riches

Grow Rich! With Peace of Mind

Adversity and Advantage

This book is affectionately dedicated to that great army of unseen students and friends of the author, throughout the world, who have found their places in the world's work through the Science of Personal Achievement philosophy which is briefly presented in these pages. The author wishes especially to express here his thanks to those faithful students who offered him encouragement during the years of poverty and struggle through which he had to pass while the Science of Personal Achievement philosophy was in the making. Finally, the author wishes to pay tribute to all who, during his lean years, tried to destroy him with ridicule and to his enemies who resorted to more violent methods, for they armed him with determination and the persistence to see his labors completed.

—NAPOLEON HILL, 1930

the
POSITIVE SIDE
of the
STREET

*A Collection of Previously
Unpublished Lectures*

NAPOLEON HILL

A POST HILL PRESS BOOK

The Positive Side of the Street:
A Collection of Previously Unpublished Lectures
© 2022 by Napoleon Hill
All Rights Reserved

ISBN: 978-1-63758-178-0
ISBN (eBook): 978-1-63758-179-7

Interior design and composition by Greg Johnson, Textbook Perfect

Post Hill Press
New York • Nashville
posthillpress.com

Published in the United States of America
1 2 3 4 5 6 7 8 9 10

Contents

Foreword

The Positive Side of the Street

Napoleon Hill was happily married, retired and living comfortably in Los Angeles in the 1950s. But he was restless, as he had been all his life. He had written dozens of books and hundreds of newspaper articles, presented and recorded an untold number of lectures, and discussed and promoted his philosophy of success on scores of radio and television programs. Napoleon came out of retirement and presented even more radio and television shows in the 1950s and wrote more books. He had a prosperous partnership with W. Clement Stone, a Chicago insurance tycoon who had coaxed him out of retirement in 1952.

His venture with Mr. Stone came to an end in 1962, but Napoleon was still not finished. He wanted to continue to teach the principles of success he had discovered over decades of study. In 1964, at age eighty, semiretired and living happily in South Carolina with his wife Annie Lou, both healthy of mind and body and with plenty of money for them to retire on, he decided to present a series of lectures in Tulsa, Oklahoma. These talks focused on all seventeen principles of success, which he called a course on the Science of Personal Achievement.

These lectures were recorded, and the recordings were only recently found by the Trustees of the Napoleon Hill Foundation. They have never been published before, in audio or print form. They are a powerful embodiment of Napoleon's success principles, and provide insight into the thinking of this great man as he neared the end of his life. He was to die six years later, in 1970.

In these lectures you will find that Mr. Hill continued to be optimistic about the future. He spoke with great inspiration and understanding about two of the important principles he had embraced later in life, positive mental attitude and cosmic habit force. He spoke expansively and eloquently based on his years of experience about the importance of accurate thinking, maintaining physical health, and, especially, going the extra mile. The lectures reveal a combination of Napoleon's ever present youthful exuberance and the wisdom gained by experience and maturity.

We are proud to present these lectures to you, and trust that they will help you along the road to your own future successes, just as they helped Napoleon Hill continue on his constant quest for achievement. We hope they will assist you to travel, as Napoleon emphasized in his lectures on the Master Mind Alliance and Positive Mental Attitude, on the positive side of the street.

—**DON M. GREEN**
CEO and Trustee of the Napoleon Hill Foundation

Introduction

The Tulsa Oklahoma Lectures

Narrator: *Introducing the Science of Personal Achievement. Welcome, ladies and gentlemen, to the world's first practical philosophy of success, by Dr. Napoleon Hill. The Science of Personal Achievement is designed to give you a richer and fuller life. It has been said that there is no surer way to success than to follow in the footsteps of those who have reached it. That is exactly what you are about to do: Take the first step with a man who has dedicated a whole lifetime to the organization and teaching of success principles. And Dr. Napoleon Hill has succeeded. So, without further delay, your teammate to success, Dr. Napoleon Hill. Dr. Hill, will you please tell our audience how you developed the Science of Personal Achievement?*

Dr. Hill: In 1908, Mr. Andrew Carnegie, then the richest man in the world and founder of the United States Steel Corporation, and builder of public libraries, commissioned me to devote twenty years to studying the causes of success and failure. He believed that the world needed a new philosophy based upon the know-how of men like himself who had learned the rules of success by the trial-and-error method.

Narrator: *Isn't it true that you interviewed Henry Ford, Thomas A. Edison, and some five hundred other outstanding businessmen of the 20th century during your research and development of the Science of Personal Achievement?*

Dr. Hill: Yes, that's true. I spent more than twenty years in interviewing America's best-known and most successful men, men like W. Clement Stone, Alexander Graham Bell, William H. Taft, former president of the United States, John Wanamaker, the Philadelphia merchant king, Woodrow Wilson, former president of the United States, Harvey Firestone, Dr. Frank Crane, F. W. Woolworth, and Theodore Roosevelt, former president of the United States. Well, don't you think that's enough? Or would you like me to continue? You know, I interviewed more than three thousand different people but only five hundred were helpful in developing this practical philosophy that is helpful to mankind in America and throughout the free world.

Narrator: *I notice in your books that you refer to the seventeen principles that make up the Science of Personal Achievement. Please name the most important of these seventeen principles.*

Dr. Hill: All seventeen of the principles are required to make the Science of Personal Achievement serve the purpose it is designed to serve. It's like a chain. If you broke a chain and took out one link, you wouldn't have a chain anymore—you'd only have two parts of a chain.

However, I will name six or seven major principles for you. Definiteness of purpose, which is the beginning of all achievement. The Master Mind, attractive personality, applied faith, going the extra mile—that is to say, doing more work and better work than you're paid to do and doing it in a pleasing mental attitude—organized endeavor, and a positive mental attitude. Any of the principles in the Science of Personal Achievement can be found in the life of Jesus of Nazareth. Certainly, he had definiteness of purpose, and it is easy to conceive that the twelve disciples were members of his Master Mind group. And the Bible records that he had self- discipline over all of his emotions, which is proof of a strong positive mental attitude.

Narrator: *In Mark 9:23 we read, "If thou canst believe, all things are possible to him that believeth."*

Dr. Hill: When one believes and uses applied faith, it enables the average person to convert failure into success. It will show one how to master the six basic fears and it will help the mind to keep positive, to build courage, and to develop initiative. Applied faith will help you to distinguish the difference between temporary defeat and failure. It will help you to gain the confidence of others. It will help one to remove all limitations from one's mind.

Narrator: *Other subjects covered in the Science of Personal Achievement consist of organized thought, controlled attention, teamwork, creative vision, and cosmic habit force. Dr. Hill, can you explain to us in fifteen or twenty words, what is cosmic habit force?*

Dr. Hill: No, you can't describe cosmic habit force in that short length of time. I read over one thousand books and spent twenty years in study before I discovered this law of nature. However, I can tell you that it is the key to the application of this philosophy and the secret of Edison's achievements in invention, and it will show you how nature uses the brain as a radio station to send and to receive vibrations of thought. Cosmic habit force is a new interpretation of the power of thought.

Narrator: *Will you please provide us with the history of the development of the Science of Personal Achievement?*

Dr. Hill: I was born down in the mountains of Virginia where the section from whence I came was famous for three things: rattlesnakes, mountain dew, and revenue officers. I never had a pair of shoes until I was ten years old. I never saw a railroad train until I was twelve. Later on, I discovered why my father named me Napoleon. I have a great-uncle—or had before he died—in Memphis, Tennessee by the name of Napoleon Hill. He was a multimillionaire cotton broker. I think if I stopped right there you'd know why my father named me Napoleon. We expected that he would leave some of his money to me on account of my having his name, but when the will was read when I was fourteen, he had left out the entire branch of Hills from whence I came, and I think that was the greatest favor that anybody ever did me, because I know what happened to the ones that did get the money. Would you mind asking what?

Audience: *What? What happened?*

Dr. Hill: Nothing. Nothing. Well, I, having had no inheritance, had to go to work, and I learned to make my own money. The next best thing that ever happened to me was when I was assigned by Andrew Carnegie to devote twenty years to the building of this philosophy. One of his conditions was that I should earn my own way as I went along without any subsidy from him. I want to tell you right now, I thought that was disastrous, but that was another blessing that came into my life. Having to earn my own way, I soon learned how to do it, and long before Mr. Carnegie died, I didn't need him anymore, financially or otherwise. I could make my own way.

Mr. Carnegie was very smart in throwing me out on my own like that. He wanted me to learn to apply this philosophy as I went along to make it work for myself, and he said a success philosopher living in a hovel without any money, and his shoes not shined, and needing a shave, is no good example of seeking success. If you want to be successful in helping other people to succeed, demonstrate that you can make your own philosophy work. And I think I have done that quite adequately, and at all levels.

Let me tell you the story of how I came to meet Andrew Carnegie. First of all, when I was in my early teens, I wanted to go away to college but didn't have any money. But I made arrangements with the Tazewell Business College to work my way through and took secretarial courses. When I finished, I looked around and I had an inspiration that has been far reaching that has affected millions of people and will affect more millions of people, some of them not yet born. I did something that has never been done before nor afterwards, as far as I know, in the way of ensuring that I would go to work for the man that I chose. I recognized that if I picked out a very successful, a very prosperous, a very wealthy man and could work for him in close contact as a secretary, that I would appropriate all of his friends and much of his knowledge and it would be worth a stupendous amount to me.

I chose General Rufus A. Ayers of Virginia. He owned a railroad, a chain of banks, a chain of sawmills, a chain of coal mines, and in addition to that, he was a senior member of one of the most important law firms in the state of Virginia. I made up my mind that General Ayers was going to have the great fortune of giving me my first job, and here is how I broke the news to him: I wrote him a letter and I said, "Dear General Ayers, I have just completed a secretarial course at Tazewell Business College and I know you will be glad to hear that I have chosen you as my first employer." Period and paragraph. "I am willing to go to work for you under the following conditions: I will work for the first three months and pay you a salary of any amount you name per month for that privilege with the understanding that if, at the end of those three months, you wish to continue my services, you'll pay me that same salary. But meanwhile, you'll allow me to put on the cuff what I'll owe you, and you can take it out of what you'll owe me if you continue my services. Sincerely, Napoleon Hill." I guess that put him on the spot, didn't it?

He didn't answer my letter. He called my father on the telephone. He said, "I want you to send that boy down; I want to look at him." He didn't say anything about employing me. I went down to this huge law office. He got up from his desk and he came around, walked all the way around me three or four times, never opened his mouth, and then he went back and sat down at his desk and he said, "I wish to ask you just one question: Did you write that letter yourself or did somebody tell you what to write?"

I said, "General Ayers, I wrote that letter myself and I meant every word of it."

He said, "That's just what I thought after I looked you over. You'll go to work tomorrow morning in the secretarial department at the regular beginning salary," a rather fabulous salary, at least fabulous in those days, of fifty dollars a month. But fifty dollars then was fifty dollars. Now, fifty dollars is not fifty dollars, it's something much less than that.

Later on, when my brother and I matriculated to Georgetown University Law School intending to become lawyers, I looked around and made a contract with a magazine to write stories about successful men. I had become a newspaper man, a cub reporter, and was fairly good at writing even then. Fortunately, I was assigned to interview Andrew Carnegie, the wealthiest man in the world at that time and known throughout the world as being the best picker of men. That's how he became successful— he knew how to surround himself with Master Mind allies that could do the things that he needed to have done. And nobody— please hear me on this—nobody ever rises above mediocrity who does not learn to use the brains of other people and sometimes the money of other people, too. We call it OPB and OPM, other people's brains and other people's money. And it takes a combination of the two, believe you me.

Andrew Carnegie gave me three hours, and when the three hours were up, he said, "This interview is just starting. Come over to the house and we'll take it up after dinner." And I was so glad that he said come on over to the house. If he'd have said, "Go over to the hotel and come back tomorrow morning," I'd have been broke because I had just about enough money in my pocket to pay my way back to Washington. After dinner, we went out to the library and he gave me one of the hardest sales talks that I had ever had or ever heard of in my whole life, about the necessity for a new philosophy that would conserve and pass on to the oncoming generations the sum total of what men like him had learned by a lifetime of trial and error method. And he said it was one of the sins of the ages that this knowledge, gained at such a tremendous price by so many men, was buried with their bones when they died. Nobody had ever organized it into a philosophy and made it available to the man on the street.

Well, I wondered why Mr. Carnegie was wasting his time on a cub reporter like me, giving me a sales talk like that. It was way beyond my capacity at that time. I was curious and I had to—I kept my ears open and my mouth shut. I kept on listening, and incidentally, that's a pretty good line. It just came to me then. My ears open and my mouth shut. It comes in handy a lot of times. Meanwhile, he told me what this philosophy would do for the man who organized it, what it would do for oncoming generations, how it would benefit people not yet born, and then he said, "I've been talking to you for three days about this new philosophy. I've told you all that I know about it, about its possibilities and its potentials. I wish to ask you a question which you will please answer with a simple yes or no, but don't answer until you make up your mind which it is. If I commission you to become the author of this philosophy, give you letters of introduction to people whose help you need, are you willing to devote twenty years to research—because that's about how long it will take—earning your own way as you go along without any subsidy from me? Yes or no?"

What would you have done if you had been sitting there in front of the richest man in the world with about enough money in your pocket to pay your way back home, who had propositioned you to go to work for twenty years without compensation and without a subsidy? What would you have said? Well, what you have in mind right now is what I had in mind, too. I knew very well that I couldn't do it. Isn't it strange that when you put an unusual opportunity before a person, a new opportunity, the chances are one thousand to one that his mind will jump to the no-can-do part of it immediately, to the negative side, to think of all the reasons in the world why he can't do it? I can think of about three right off the bat. First of all, I didn't have enough money to carry me for twenty years. Second place, I didn't have enough education to deal with these successful men that I'd have to deal with all over the United States and in other countries. And in the third place—and this was about the most serious of all—I was not absolutely too sure about the meaning of that word "philosophy" that Mr. Carnegie had been kicking around for three days and nights.

So you can imagine what a fantastic thing it was, a young man with very little education sitting in front of this great man who had offered him an opportunity such as never has come to any other author at any time in the civilization of man. No author, as far as I've been able to tell, has ever had the cooperation and the collaboration of over five hundred outstanding men to help create a literary work of any sort. That was the kind of opportunity that was facing me.

Here is an important thing I want to call to your attention. I didn't know this at the time, but I learned about it later. After briefing me for three days and nights on the potential of this philosophy, on how it could be organized, on what it would do, Mr. Carnegie made up his mind that when he put the question to me, he would allow me only sixty seconds in which to say yes or no. Sixty seconds, that's all. I didn't see it, but he's sitting there with a stopwatch behind his desk, timing me. It took me exactly twenty-nine seconds to make up my mind that I would accept. I had thirty-one seconds between me and losing an opportunity such as has never been undertaken by another author. I have never known of any author in any field having so much help, so much guidance given and supplied, without money and without price.

I was ready to go back to Washington, and Mr. Carnegie then did another thing. If you don't get anything out of this talk except what I'm now about to tell you, it might well change your entire destiny, and through you, the destiny of many other people. Mr. Carnegie said, "Well, Napoleon, twenty years is a long time and I have given you a pretty tough assignment, and you have accepted it. I want to warn you now that you're going to have many temptations along the way, long before you complete your research, to quit because that's the easiest thing that a weakling can do is quit. I don't think you're a weakling—if I had thought so, I would not have given you the opportunity—but I do know that you need something to bridge over your temptations to quit, if and when they do come. I am now going to give you a formula that will enable you to condition your mind so thoroughly that nothing in the world can stop you from going ahead and completing the task I have assigned you."

I was taking all this down in shorthand. He said, "I want you to write very slowly and I want you to underscore every word that I speak now. And here's the message that I want you to repeat to yourself at least twice a day, once just before you go to bed at night and once just after you get up. Looking at yourself in a mirror, you're talking to Napoleon Hill now, mind you, and here's what you say to him: Andrew Carnegie, I'm not only going to equal your achievements in life but I'm going to challenge you at the post and pass you at the grandstand."

I threw my pencil down and I said, "Now, Mister Carnegie, let's be realistic. You know very well I'm not going to be able to do that."

At that time, Mr. Carnegie was rated as a billionaire, probably the first and maybe the only billionaire this country has ever created, as far as I know. He said, "Why, of course I know you're not going to be able to do that unless and until you believe it, but if you believe it, you will." But he said, "Let me ask you to do this: Try it out for thirty days. Will you do that?"

I said, "Yes, that's a reasonable request; I certainly will," but I had the fingers on both hands crossed. I knew doggone well it wouldn't work. The idea of a youngster in his early twenties promising to equal and outdo the achievements of a man who had reached the stage of a billionaire; why it was so ridiculous it wasn't even funny. It even scared me. I thought Mr. Carnegie had lost his mind. I came very near walking out on him. It was just something that was too good to be true. But I promised. And when I got back to Washington—my brother and I had an apartment— when I went to go over this adventure with him, I didn't want my brother to know what a big fool I'd made of myself, because I had some news to break to him that was not going to be good anyway. I had agreed to pay the expenses of the two of us through school and I was going to have to tell him that I was dropping out and he'd have to earn his own way. I went into the bathroom and I closed the door real tight and I got real close up to the glass and almost whispered this formula.

As I turned around, in my mind's eye I saw the real Napoleon Hill standing there, and I said, "You darn liar, you know very well you're not going to be able to do that." Only darn is not the word I used. It was a much more definite and stronger word. And I felt like a fool, like a thief going through a thing like that—a farce. And that's just what it seemed like. "Well," I said, "Well, after all, you promised Mr. Carnegie; go ahead and try it."

For the first week or, just about the first week, I had that attitude or feeling like I was doing something foolish. And then all of a sudden, about the beginning of the second week, something inside of me said, "Why don't you change your mental attitude about this? Do you realize if Andrew Carnegie is the richest man in the world, and he is known all over the world as the best picker of men in the world, and if he chose you to do a job like this, he must have found something in you that you didn't know was there. Why don't you change your mental attitude?"

And ladies and gentlemen, I started to change my mental attitude. If I hadn't have done so, I wouldn't be standing here talking to you today, and I wouldn't be talking to millions of people in this and other countries of the free world through my books, if I hadn't have changed my mental attitude and become positive instead of negative. I started to repeat this in earnest, and by the end of the month I not only believed that I'd catch up with Mr. Carnegie, but I knew that I would excel him, and believe you me when I tell you that I have long since attained that objective. And I'll tell you why I've attained it.

Mr. Carnegie made twenty or twenty-five millionaires at the most. The millionaires that I have had the privilege of making, they're legion; they're all over the world. But that's not the main claim for my having outranked Mr. Carnegie. I have brought men and women together in a spirit of understanding that didn't exist. I help men and women to find themselves in all walks of life. I have saved men and women from suicide by helping them to find themselves. I have done for the world things that Mr. Carnegie never did do. And not only that, but what I have done has been recorded, it's been tested. It's being taken to the free world, and it's going to benefit millions of people who are not yet born.

I look forward to tomorrow and all the other tomorrows that are to come with hope of that achievement, with hope of living to see this philosophy spread to the entire free world, and I have faith absolutely that I will live to see it.

the
POSITIVE SIDE
of the
STREET

Chapter 1

Definiteness of Purpose

Narrator: *We are now at the beginning of the seventeen principles, the starting point of all achievement. It would be quite confusing to start off on a journey to nowhere, that is, not knowing where you were going. But Dr. Hill, isn't that what the vast majority of people today are doing with their precious lives?*

Dr. Hill: Absolutely. Ninety-eight out of every one hundred people are going round and round like a goldfish in a bowl, coming back to the place from which they started empty-handed. Let me tell you some of the benefits of definiteness of purpose.

1. Definiteness of purpose automatically develops self-reliance, personal initiative, imagination, enthusiasm, self-discipline, and concentration of effort, all of these being prerequisites for success.

2. It induces one to budget one's time and to plan day-to-day endeavors which lead to the attainment of one's major purpose.

3. It makes one more alert in recognizing opportunities related to the object of one's major purpose, and it inspires the courage to embrace and act upon these opportunities.

4. It inspires confidence in one's integrity and character and attracts the favorable attention of other people. The man who knows where he is going and is determined to get there will always find willing helpers to cooperate with him.

5. It opens the way for the full exercise of that state of mind known as faith by making the mind positive and freeing the mind from the limitations of fear and doubt and discouragement and indecision and procrastination—the greatest of all benefits.

6. It makes one success conscious and protects one against the influence of a failure consciousness.

Here are some examples of men who have risen to high places as a result of definiteness of purpose. Take Walter Chrysler, for example. He started out as a mechanic and he wound up the head of a very large and successful automobile company. Then there was Thomas A. Edison, who chose as his profession the business of inventing. And there was Henry Ford, who built the first successful automobiles in the United States; and Andrew Carnegie, my sponsor; and F. W. Woolworth, who made himself rich by operating five and ten cent stores. And then there were Henry J. Kaiser and Edwin C. Barnes, an associate of Thomas A. Edison.

All of these men owe their success mainly to following the principle of definiteness of purpose—knowing where they wanted to go, having a plan for getting there, and keeping eternally at it in applying this plan.

Narrator: *Dr. Hill, wouldn't you say that every living person needs to master this principle? By that I mean, it is a necessity for the housewife, college student, high school student, the beauty shop operator, the stenographer, just as it is a necessity for the salesman or the business executive?*

Dr. Hill: It's absolutely impossible for anybody to succeed at any level of life without definiteness of purpose. You have to know where you're going, you have to know why you're going, and you have to be determined to get there. This applies to people in all callings. There's no exception, absolutely. No one has ever been known to succeed without definiteness of purpose. That is, above mediocrity. Of course, you can go out and run a peanut stand without definiteness of purpose, but you wouldn't get anywhere beyond that if you didn't lift your sights up and make up your mind that you wanted to do something greater than running a peanut stand.

Listen now to the advantages of having a definite major purpose. Each point will be given slowly in condensed outline form. This will help you fully understand the foundation for personal achievement.

- Ideas are the only assets which have no fixed values
- The greatest of all motives is love
- The starting point of all personal achievement is the adoption of a definite major purpose and a definite plan for its attainment

- The power of thought is the only thing over which any human being has complete unquestionable control
- Any dominating desire, plan, or purpose which is backed by faith is taken over by the subconscious mind and acted upon immediately
- Definiteness of purpose makes your mind more alert to recognize opportunities related to the object of your major purpose and it inspires the necessary courage to act upon these opportunities when they appear
- The six major qualities developed by having a definite purpose in life are:

  1. Self-reliance
  2. Personal initiative
  3. Imagination
  4. Enthusiasm
  5. Self-discipline
  6. Concentration of effort

Andrew Carnegie said that the act of writing down one's major purpose forces one to be specific as to its nature. The act of habitual reading fixes the nature of the purpose in the mind where it can be picked up by the subconscious mind and acted upon.

The nine basic motives which inspire all voluntary action are:

1. The emotion of love
2. The emotion of sex
3. The desire for material gain
4. The desire for self-preservation
5. The desire for freedom of body and mind

6. The desire for self-expression and recognition
7. The desire for life after death
8. The desire for revenge
9. The emotion of fear

Our real wealth consists of the intangible power of thought. It reflects itself in broader vision, wider horizons, greater ambitions, and initiative.

The nine ingredients of genius are:

1. Definiteness of purpose
2. Applied faith
3. Enthusiasm
4. Imagination
5. Motive
6. Personal initiative backed by intense action
7. The habit of going the extra mile
8. Forming a master mind alliance with other people
9. Positive mental attitude

Think now for a moment about the differences between the conscious mind and the subconscious mind. The conscious mind is where reasoning or thinking occurs. It is where deliberation and weighing of facts takes place. It is capable of analyzing information and data which comes before it, and one of its functions is to act as the guardian to the passageway to the subconscious.

The subconscious mind is the natural uncultivated part of the mind which comes as standard equipment at birth. It does not think, reason, or deliberate. It acts instinctively and responds to the basic emotions of humankind. The conscious mind is the architect; the subconscious mind is the vast warehouse from which may be requisitioned the mental material for the construction project. The conscious mind makes the plans and decides what shall be done. The subconscious mind develops the power to carry out the plans.

Let's look at the difference between a mere wish and a burning desire. A mere wish is only a hope with little or no thought given to the payment of the price necessary for its attainment, whereas a burning desire is a fixed want or desire that is so definite and associated with such powerful motives that it becomes an obsession for which you are willing to pay the necessary price to get it.

With these thoughts in mind on the importance of defining and establishing your definite major purpose, I believe that you will understand better what Ralph Waldo Emerson meant in his description of an idea: "One single idea may have greater weight than the labor of all men, animals, and engines for a century."

Now I want to tell you something that's very close to my heart about definiteness of purpose. I learned a lot about it long before I ever met Andrew Carnegie. When I was ten years of age, my mother died, and two years later my father brought in a stepmother. Long before she got there, my in-laws had coached me and my little brother to hate that woman who was coming in to take my mother's place. And we had done a wonderful job of getting ready to hate her. My father brought her home. All the relatives were there and they were standing around. My father took her around and introduced her to all the uncles and aunts, and he said, "Over here in the corner, Martha, is your son, Napoleon, the meanest boy in Wise County, and I wouldn't be at all surprised if he starts throwing rocks at you by tomorrow morning." I tightened up my arms and I said, "You're darn right." I'll show that woman something. And I meant to do just that. She came over and put her hand under my chin and lifted my head way up and looked squarely into my eyes, and she turned around and made a speech that has reverberated around this world, has influenced millions of people already and will influence millions of others for the better.

She said, "You're wrong about this boy. You're just as wrong as you can be. He's not the meanest boy in Wise County; he's probably just the smartest boy who hasn't found out yet what to do with his smartness." I knew then and there that my stepmother and I were going to get along all right. That was the first time in my life that anybody had ever said anything kind about me. I was a bad boy. I had a revolver, I used it effectively, and everybody in the whole mountain section was afraid of me, and not without cause. My stepmother went to work on me. She had me trade in that revolver for a typewriter and taught me to type. And in no time, I had twenty-six newspapers as my employers. I wrote a newsletter from those mountain sections for those newspapers, and when we didn't have news, ladies and gentlemen, believe you me, I made it up.

About a month after my stepmother came, she dropped her denture one morning and broke it. Up until that time, I had never heard of such thing as a denture. Of course, I've heard a lot about them since. My father went over—he had a blacksmith shop and a little country store and a post office. An all-around tinkerer, you might say. And oh yes, what purported to be a little farm among the rocks where they put me to work when I didn't do just what they wanted me to do. Oh, what work it was. He reassembled the two pieces of this upper plate, looked at it for a moment and said,

"Martha, you know, I believe I can make a set of teeth." She ran over there and threw her arms around him and said, "Well, I know you can make a set of teeth." I thought, what a woman. What a woman. My old man make a set of teeth? He could shoe a horse, I knew, because I'd seen him do it. But teeth?

About three weeks after that, when I came home from school, I smelled the most peculiar odor when I got in the yard. When I got in the house, there was a queer little kettle sitting over the fire. I said to my stepmother, "What is that?" She said, "That's a vulcanizer. Your father sent away to the dental supply house, he got the materials, he made me a set of teeth and they're in there cooking." And I thought, "My gosh, what a woman." Of course, this plate was being cooked under pressure, and my father took this little kettle down to the creek and cooled it off and took out this great hunk of plaster of Paris, trimmed away the outside of it, took a piece of emery cloth, and dressed the plate down. And I knew they'd never get into my stepmother's mouth; it looked too big. But he put it in and it fit almost perfectly, and she wore it for three years.

Next time I came home from school, there was a neat hand-painted sign on our front door: Dr. J. M. Hill, Dentist. By George, she'd made a dentist out of him overnight, without the details of his going to school or taking an examination or getting a license. He went down to the blacksmith shop and he made himself some tools to pull teeth with, and you should see them. Oh boy, they did the business. He loaded this stuff in a pair of saddle pockets and started practicing dentistry over in eastern Kentucky and southwest Virginia and down in Tennessee. Well, just in no time we were in the money—really in the money—making fifty dollars or sixty dollars a month. That went on for about three years. One day the local justice of the peace came down with a law book under his arm. He said, "Look here, Doctor Hill, Section 540 of the Code of Virginia says that you have to have a license to practice dentistry, and if you don't have it, you're liable to go to jail." He and my stepmother went into a caucus and reached the understanding that my father would ride out to the county seat and see a lawyer. Late in the afternoon, I saw him riding down the valley coming home, and I knew by the way he was thumping on the horse that he had done just what 999 out of every 1,000 people generally always do. He'd accepted the problem as something he couldn't do anything about. The lawyer said he had to have taken an examination to be a dentist, and my father came to the conclusion he didn't have education enough to take an examination. He dismounted and he said, "Well, Martha, it's all over. The lawyer says I have to take an examination, and you know I don't have enough education to do that."

The average woman would have walked away and said it was just too bad, we'll try something else, but that wasn't the way my stepmother operated. If she'd have operated like that, I wouldn't be standing here talking to you today, and I wouldn't be talking to millions of people all over the world because there would have been no Napoleon Hill. She said, "Now look here, Doctor Hill, I haven't made a dentist out of you to have you let me down. If you have to go away to college and learn how to take an examination just like the others, then that's exactly what you'll do." And I thought, my goodness, what a woman. What a woman. My old man go away to college? Why, they wouldn't let him on the campus, let alone matriculate.

You know what she did? I'm talking to you now about somebody who moves with definiteness of purpose and didn't know the opposite of definiteness of purpose. She sent my father down to the Louisville Dental College, put him through college for four years with the life insurance money of her former husband, and made him one of the most outstanding dentists in southwest Virginia. He became one of the most prominent dentists probably in the whole state of Virginia. That's how she operated. That's how anybody will operate who gets a hold of this principle of definiteness of purpose the way that it's capable of being used. If you didn't have anything else in the world except this principle and knew exactly what you wanted and stood by your guns, you could almost forget the other sixteen principles. It's just that important.

Chapter 2

Master Mind Alliance

Dr. Hill: Good morning, everybody. And it is a good morning. You know the master mind principle is one of the most difficult to get across to the beginner. A great many people confuse it with cooperation. Cooperation means the coordination of effort between two or more people, but the master mind principle means the coordination of effort between two or more people towards a single goal in a spirit of perfect harmony. And I would emphasize those last two words, perfect harmony, because there can be no master mind where that harmony does not exist.

When I went to interview the great Andrew Carnegie in 1908, the first question I asked him was if he could describe to me, in a very brief sentence, how he attained his success. He said, "Well, before I undertake to answer that question, define your term 'success.' What do you mean by that?"

I said, "Well, Mister Carnegie, I have reference to your fortune, of course."

He said, "I thought that's what you meant. If that's all you want to know, I can tell you in a very few moments how I got it. I surrounded myself with a master mind alliance."

I thought, well, Mr. Carnegie is going to tell me now that he has a master mind. But instead he said, "It doesn't consist of one mind, but it consists of the minds of some twenty men whose education, experience, background, and influence combined and directed to a definite end in a spirit of perfect harmony have been responsible for my fortune."

I said, "Mister Carnegie, who are these men?" And he went ahead and described them. One was his chief chemist, one was his chief legal advisor, one was his plant works manager, and so on down the line. He named every one of them and told me what each man did. Then he said, "The sum total of the ability of these men is responsible entirely for what you call my success."

I said, "Well, pray tell me, Mister Carnegie, what do you do?"

He said, "I have the hardest job of all. My job is to keep these men busy pulling together in a spirit of perfect harmony."

While I was there with Mr. Carnegie, I learned from one of his associates an astounding experience that he had in connection with the master mind. Mr. Carnegie wanted to employ the best chemist in the world, and he sent out talent scouts all over the world and finally located what they believed to be the finest and the ablest chemist in the whole world, and he was then employed by the great Krupp Gun works in Germany. They made a five year contract with him at a fabulous salary per year and brought him over here, and within six months they had to pay him off for the whole five years and send him back because he had one quality that made it intolerable for Mr. Carnegie to keep him as a member of his master mind alliance, and that quality was that he had an unpleasant disposition. He literally exuded negative attitude, and when he walked into the master mind group when they were having a meeting, they wanted to hit him in the face with a brick before he opened his mouth. You've seen people of that type where they didn't have to say anything—you just had to get close enough to them to pick up their vibrations and you wanted to slap them in the face or do something else. Mr. Carnegie said, "When you form the master mind, you can make mistakes in selecting your members." "And what do you do in that case, Mister Carnegie?"

He said, "We either cure the situation or kill it, one or the other. We first try to cure it, and if we can't cure it, then we kill it."

I asked, "Does that apply to every member of your master mind alliance?"

He said, "It applies to every member. Under no circumstances would I tolerate a man working in my master mind group who did not have absolute sympathy in connection with the objective of the group and who did not work in harmony, who did not subordinate personal beliefs and personal interests for the good of the whole."

It has been said that the Nazarene's power came largely as a result of his master mind alliance with his twelve disciples. And it's only a matter of history known to all of us that when one of these disciples, Judas Iscariot, went sour, the Master met with the supreme catastrophe of his life. I've seen that duplicated over and over and over again in business and in human relationships during my fifty-five years of experience with this subject. I've seen businesses—fine, wonderful businesses—go down because some one or two men at the top echelon of the organization got to bickering with one another, sometimes over small matters. I've seen it happen in homes where a man and his wife would start in a small way to poke fun at one another, so to speak, and then it went from bad to worse and got along to where they got into the habit of throwing mental darts at one another. Then the next step is divorce court.

The master mind alliance is one of the most powerful parts of this entire philosophy. No business can long go on and succeed unless there is harmony at the top. It's not so bad where there's lack of harmony down toward the bottom, but when there's lack of harmony at the top, you cannot succeed no matter how meritorious your objective may be, no matter how much ability you may have, no matter what your intention may be. If you do not work together in a spirit of harmony, if you do not resolve your differences—your petty differences or your major differences—if you do not resolve them and get them out of the way, they will destroy you just as sure as I'm standing here talking to you. There's no alternative.

It may interest all of you to know of my alliance with Franklin D. Roosevelt during those hectic days of 1933. I first met him when he was assistant secretary of the Navy, and I did a lot of work for him at that time. Later on, when he became Governor of New York, I helped him on various occasions to do confidential work. When he went to the White House in 1933, we were in a state of chaos and frustration in this country such as we had never known before. I was one of the first men that set forth to come down and work on a confidential basis, and we built one of the finest, one of the most powerful, and one of the most far reaching master mind organizations that this or any other country has ever known. In a matter of months, we had taken those scare headlines off of the newspapers about business depression and replaced them with headlines about business recovery. In other words, we took this nation from the negative side of the street onto the positive side of the street, and we started talking about the things that we had that were right instead of the things that we had that were wrong. That's a mighty good rule for anybody to follow at any level of life. Find out what is good and talk about that, deal with that more than that which is not right.

Well, what did we do in building a master mind alliance for the President? First of all, we built a coalition between both houses of Congress, and in a matter of thirty days there were no Republicans and no Democrats and no Socialists in the Congress—just Americans dedicated to helping the President of the United States bring this country out of a state of chaos. We crossed party lines. There were no such things as party lines. I don't think that ever happened before; I don't think it has ever happened since. It would be a mighty fine thing if it happened along about now.

Then we had the majority of the newspaper publishers, and they also crossed party lines. Regardless of their political affiliations or attitudes, every single solitary one of them got back of the President of the United States and started to sell the merits of the United States to their readers. They did a wonderful job. I think every bulletin that I sent out, that I wrote, was published in every paper wherever it was sent. I don't think a single paper turned down any of the material that I prepared. They did a wonderful job. And then the radio station operators—of course, television hadn't come along—it still had on short pants at that time—but radio was going strong, and we had those radio station operators going on the air with our bulletins, talking about the merits of the United States of America instead of the demerits.

And then fourth, the churches of all denominations—I tell you what, that was a beautiful thing to see, the Catholics and the Protestants and the Jews and all the others going into their pulpits and selling the United States of America to the people, emphasizing the things in our country that were right. They did a magnificent job. What a wonderful thing it would be if all the churches reunited again and started selling the things in this country that are good and letting the devil take care of himself the best he could.

Then we reached the leaders of both major political parties. You may or may not know that in Washington, there's a relatively little handful of men in the upper and lower house that rule the whole outfit. We happened to know who those leaders were, and we had them over to the White House for luncheons time and time again until those leaders were working together in a spirit of harmony, a masterful job.

Last, but not least, a majority of the American people—we had them talking and thinking in terms of the things in this country that were still left that were good instead of going back to the days when we're talking about the things that were bad. And I don't need to tell you what the result was.

Those of us who were close to Franklin D. Roosevelt and a lot of the American people felt that he was sent straight from heaven to do a job in a great emergency. One of the notable things about this country is that in times of major emergencies, there has come out of the rank and file of the people a great man to meet those emergencies. During the revolution, it was George Washington. During the war between the states, it was Abraham Lincoln.

Speaking of master mind alliances, my twenty years of research under the direction of Andrew Carnegie constituted perhaps one of the most outstanding master mind alliances that any author at any time on any subject has ever had the privilege of benefiting himself by. I had over five hundred of the most outstanding brains of this country working with me at an intimate level, giving me the benefit of what they had learned by the trial and error method about the rules and principles of success. I think perhaps what I got from Mr. Thomas A. Edison alone would have made a wonderful philosophy by itself if I hadn't have had any of the others.

I worked very closely with Mr. Edison for about eleven years. The first time I went to see Mr. Edison, I went with a letter of introduction from Andrew Carnegie, and I had heard that when Mr. Edison was working on the incandescent electric lamp, he failed over ten thousand different times with ten thousand different experiments before he found the thing that would work. When I asked him about it, he said, "Would you like to see the logbooks where I registered on every page of every book an experiment that wouldn't work?" He took me back into his laboratory and there were two stacks of logbooks that high, perhaps each one with 250 pages in it, and on every page of every book there was something he had tried that wouldn't work.

Can you imagine how many times the average man has to fail before he quits and says, "I guess I can't do this," or "I guess I'll do something else?" Give a guess, will you please? How many times—I'm talking about the average man now. How many times? Well, how many times would you have to fail before you'd quit? When you go into the field and you meet a little opposition from somebody who doesn't want this philosophy, are you going to turn in your kit and then quit? If you're an average person, that's exactly what you'll do.

Mr. Edison failed ten thousand times. I said, "Mr. Edison, if you hadn't found the answer to the incandescent electric lamp, what would you be doing right now?"

He said, "What I would be doing right now—I'd be in my laboratory working instead of out here wasting my time talking with you." I think he meant just what he said. Then he turned to me with a twinkle in his eye, and he said, "You know, I had to succeed because I ran out of things that wouldn't work." Wasn't that an astounding thing? When you analyze that, it brings you right down to the one thing that every person who rises above mediocrity must do if he succeeds—run out of things that won't work. Most people don't even start using the things that won't work, let alone run out of them. They quit before they start and say, "Well, I never could do that. It's alright for Napoleon Hill to talk about wealth and success and so forth; he's got it. He doesn't need it. But I don't have it." I've heard them say that very thing.

If you adopt Mr. Edison's philosophy and keep on keeping on until you run out of things that won't work, you'll discover the principle—the one thing that enabled me to get the assignment from the great Andrew Carnegie. Mr. Carnegie, for a number of years, had been looking for a man to organize the Science of Personal Achievement who had to have a number of qualities, among them one I'm now going to tell you about. He knew that if the man who undertook the job did not have this quality, he would never succeed. What would you say is the one quality without which no man ever rises above mediocrity, if you had to narrow it down to just one quality? What would you say it is? Honesty? Well, I knew a lot of people in the poorhouse down in Wise County—every one of them was honest. That's the reason they got in the poorhouse—they didn't have anything else but honesty. You'll starve to death on honesty if you don't have something to go along with it.

Mr. Carnegie was looking for a man who, when the going became hard, as he knew it would in twenty years of unsubsidized research, would keep on keeping on instead of quitting. In other words, that word "quit." There are two words in the dictionary that I dislike thoroughly. One is the word "impossible" and the other is the word "quit." I've had to deal with both of them all down through the years—men who were ready to quit or considered the task impossible. One example was when I said to my publisher, my first publisher in 1928, "I'm prepared to confer upon you an honor and a benefit second only to that conferred upon me by Andrew Carnegie by allowing you to become the first publisher of my first work," paraphrasing that, ladies and gentlemen. I met with resistance. I am prepared to say to you that every one of you who qualifies and who allies himself with this gigantic world-wide undertaking and carries out the mission in confidence and in good faith, every single solitary one of you has a much better opportunity at this level to get from life whatever you want than I had when I started with Andrew Carnegie because all of the groundwork has been done. I have known many wonderful authors in many fields who wore out their shoe leather and their patience trying to get their books or material across who never made it to first base. Only one time in my whole life—only one time—did I feel it necessary to seek out a publisher. After my first works were published, the publishers beat a path to my door. But that first publisher was hard to convince.

Somebody sent a copy of *Think and Grow Rich* to Mahatma Gandhi in India. He thought so much of it that he wanted to have it widely distributed throughout India because he wanted to break up that caste system in India. But before he did anything about it, he sent an emissary over here to the United States, and they put me under twenty-four hour a day surveillance for three months. They wanted to know whether I was a fake, a fraud, or a ghost writer, or the real McCoy, and they employed the Pinkerton Detective Agency. They took me to bed and they got me up without my knowing it. I remember on one evening, I was entertaining a young lady at the famous Stork Club in New York—or maybe infamous Stork Club to some—and the man who was tailing me couldn't get a table close enough to hear what was going on, so he employed a lip reader. Three tables away, a lip reader took down every word that was said by my guest and myself. I was glad I was saying the right thing. Later on, one of the men who tailed me during that campaign became a student of mine, and we became intimately acquainted, and he said, "This is just too good to keep." And he brought down the record and showed it to me. He was not supposed to do that. It was a stack of reports that high. I read them, and there wasn't a single mistake in the entire report. It was the most marvelous job of reporting I've ever seen in my life. Never seen anything to equal it.

Mahatma Gandhi, when that report went back to him, ordered the books published in India, first *Think and Grow Rich* and subsequently every book that I've ever published. They were picked up there by a publisher in Brazil, translated into the Portuguese language, and widely distributed throughout Brazil and all other countries where the Portuguese language is spoken predominantly. It went from there to Canada, where the books were published, and then to Australia and then to Spain and now to Japan.

I say to you, unless it were true that the power back of this philosophy is a miraculous power, this simply couldn't have happened; I'm quite sure of it. I'm quite sure that I've had some invisible powerful aid along the way that's kept me alive and kept me going in refining and preparing this great philosophy and in helping to take it to the people.

Incidentally, I have a system—a very wonderful system—for applying this philosophy in my own life, and I think you'll be interested in knowing what this system is. And you may want to adopt it or some portions of it. It's not accidental that at the age of eighty I have the health that I have. I'm in good trim mentally and physically. It's not accidental. It's not accidental that I have, materially speaking, everything in this world that I need and have it in abundance. And if I needed more, all I have to do is reach out my hands and close my hands when it comes in because I've already earned it. That's not accidental. It came about as a result of a system that I have of dealing with Napoleon Hill. And I want to tell you he's been the hardest rascal to deal with that I've ever met in my life. I literally had to rebuild him. I think if you'll be honest with yourself, you'll find the same thing in your past. Your hardest problem is to get yourself under control and to keep yourself under control.

Before I tell you what my system is, I want to tell you about one of the most interesting master mind allies that I had. His name was Dr. Elmer R. Gates of Chevy Chase, Maryland. Andrew Carnegie knew about Dr. Gates and about his marvelous system of drawing upon the invisible powers of the universe, and he sent me to see Dr. Gates with a letter of introduction. When I got there, I presented my letter and his secretary said, "I'm sorry, but Doctor

Gates is not available for the next three hours. He's now sitting for ideas."

I said, "I beg your pardon?"

"He is now sitting for ideas."

I said, "Where is he sitting?" I looked around.

"Well," she said, "only Doctor Gates would be able to answer that one. He has a secret room into which he disappears when he wants to sit for ideas. You can come back in three hours, or you can wait if you like."

I said, "I'm going to wait. I don't want to get out of this place until I see Doctor Gates." In about two hours and a half, he came out, and I told him about my conversation with his secretary.

He said, "Would you like to see where I sit for ideas?"

I said, "I certainly would." He took me back into a room about 12'x12'. The walls had been insulated to cut out all sound. There was nothing in that room but a table against the wall, an electric switch over the table, and a bunch of scratch pads and some pencils on the table. And he explained to me that when he—and by the way, he was a great inventor, a great scientist—wants to solve a problem and there is an unknown quality or quantity, x, that he hasn't found, he goes into his concentration room, shuts off the lights, shuts off the sound, and concentrates his mind upon that which he wants to discover. Sometimes he gets the answer within a matter of minutes, sometimes in a matter of hours, and once in a while, not at all. When sitting for ideas, he is letting his subconscious mind contact him with the source of knowledge necessary to give him the answer to his problem. By that method he has created over 250 inventions which have been registered in the Patent Office of the United States.

I became intrigued by Dr. Gates's experiment because, if he had not been a man of great achievement, I would have written him off as a long-haired nut, as we sometimes call them. But he was a man of great achievement, and I can always learn from the man who has done more than I have in life. I started to study his system, and I came up with a system of my own, which I would now like to describe for you.

First of all, I created these invisible entities—I call them my invisible guides—each one assigned to do for me automatically, night and day, a job that I need to have done in order to carry out my objective in life. The number one of these invisible guides is the guide to sound physical health. His job is to keep my body eternally in good shape. The moment I lay the carcass down at night and go to sleep, he goes to work on me. And when I get up in the morning, I feel like a million dollars, or maybe two or three million, depending on what I'm thinking about. I think I needn't go into any detail as to whether or not he is doing a good job. You can take a look at me and come in contact with him and make your own decision. When I tell you that I've only been sick— really sick—once in my life, you know that I have had an unusual system to keep well. If all the doctors had to depend upon men like myself, believe you me they'd have to change their profession. They certainly would.

Number two is the guide to financial prosperity. He has put me in a position where I don't need anything at all of a material nature that I can't buy. I don't have any debts, I don't have any mortgages on our home, I don't have any mortgages on our car, and I don't buy cars or anything else on installment plans. We have funds in so many different institutions I wouldn't be able to name all of them. We're not as rich as Carnegie, but we're as rich as we need to be. We have enough for absolute security in old age, which gives you a wonderful feeling to know that as old age comes along, you don't have to go to the poorhouse or depend upon relatives. So the guide to financial prosperity is doing all right.

Number three is the guide to peace of mind. His job is to keep my mind eternally free from all of the causes and the effects of fear and worry. You know fear and worry killed off more talented people and untalented people than all the other subjects combined, in all probability. Fear and worry. I don't have any fears. I used to have a flock of them before I adopted this system, but I don't have them anymore; they're all gone.

The next two are twins. They are the guides to hope and faith. They give me hope for what's going to happen to me in the future in connection with my aims and purposes and, backing up that hope, the faith in my ability to do it. I want to tell you that they are doing a good job. I have hopes of seeing this philosophy in every country upon the face of this earth, not only in just the free countries of the world but also widely distributed in all the under-privileged nations of this country where men are being enslaved because of the lack of the application of a philosophy like this.

The next two are also twins. They are the guides to love and romance. When I speak of love, I speak of that great emotion in its widest and broadest and most divine application. Love and romance. I can find romance in everything that crosses my path, whether it's pleasant or unpleasant. If it's unpleasant, I romance the idea that I'll find that seed of equivalent benefit and I'll make use of it. Love. What a marvelous thing it is to have a feeling of love in your heart. I have been accused of carrying this emotion to extremes on some occasions, but I don't think so.

Mrs. Hill and I were driving out in the mountains of California about ten years ago, and we saw on the side of the road an enormous rattlesnake coiled and ready to strike. Annie Lou saw it about the same time I did. She said, "Hit it. Hit it." Well, I didn't hit it. I wheeled around and entirely bypassed it. She said, "Why didn't you hit it?" I said, "My dear, the reason I didn't hit it: It's on its own ground, it's doing its own business, and that's exactly what you and I are going to do. We're not going to kill something that doesn't concern us." That's the attitude that I'll take toward a rattlesnake or anything else that won't bother me or some of my friends. I wouldn't bother it. In other words, I changed my whole attitude, not only toward my fellow men but also toward every living creature on the face of this earth.

I'm not as extreme as one of the professors up at Harvard University when I was lecturing there in 1922. I made the acquaintance of one of the professors who I thought was quite a nut. We were walking one evening in a swampy section of the campus where mosquitoes were bad, and one of them lit over on his hand and began to bore into his skin. I reached over to hit it and he said, "Oh, don't hit that. He's got to live, too." I said, "You better not let your mosquito get over on my hand, Professor, because I'll sure slap him down."

The next one is a lately acquired member of my imaginary family. He's the guide to patience. I acquired that during the past ten years with experiences that required a lot of patience. Thank heavens that's one of the things I can count on that I got out of those ten years that has been beneficial—patience. Patience enables you to time things properly, not just to plant the seed today and go back tomorrow and dig it up to see if it's going to germinate or not. If you plant your seed with faith in the right kind of soil at the right time of year and know that the seed is sound, you can forget about it because nature takes over at that point. For every seed of wheat that you put in the ground under the proper circumstances, nature will bring you back five hundred or six hundred grains to compensate you for your effort. And it works in other places just the same as in soil.

The next one, number eight—I just want to see if you're keeping up with me. I know you were all the time. Number nine is the guide to overall wisdom, and his job is to keep me benefited by every experience that touches my life, whether it's good or bad, positive or negative. Everything that touches my life is grist for my mill. I make some use out of it. If it's an unpleasant experience, I try to surround myself with enough protection to see that the same thing won't happen again. Believe you me, we all need that kind of a protection, not to let things that happen to you that are unpleasant happen over and over and over again. I like to remember that very interesting Chinese proverb which says, "If a man injure me once, shame on him, but if that man injure me twice, shame on me."

The last one is an interesting one. His name is Norm Hill, and that's a combination of my wife's maiden name and mine. He's my roving ambassador. His job is to do the things that have not been specifically assigned to the other nine. For example, I'm in my car and I'm driving downtown and in these traffic conditions nowadays, in almost every city it's difficult to get a parking spot. But I never have any trouble in getting a parking spot because I send Norm Hill ahead, and he has a place cleared out for me by the time I get there.

A couple of years ago, I was telling one of my neighbors about this Norm Hill fellow, and he said, "Well, isn't that interesting?"

I said, "By the way, if I wanted to go down to the bank on Friday afternoon—banks close at 1:00 PM Friday—and I didn't have but a few minutes to get down there, not time enough to go over to a parking lot, which is four or five blocks away from the bank where I do business, I would send Norm Hill ahead, and when I got there, he'd have me a place right in front of the bank." He said, "That reminds me, I have got to go to the bank. Would you mind letting me see how Norm Hill works?" I said, "Hop in; we don't have much time." And I drove pretty fast. And when we got down in front of the South Carolina National Bank, sure enough, there were no parking spots. Every place on both sides of the street was filled. I stopped my car about three car lengths back of the front of the bank and this man said, "Uh-huh, Norm Hill must have walked and I noticed you drove pretty fast." I said, "Don't you worry about Norm; he'll be here in good time." Within the time that I've been telling you the story, a man came out of the bank and got in the car right in front of the bank and drove off, and the one after him got in the next car, and now there were two spots. I said, "See there? One to compensate me for my belief and one to show you that you ought to think twice before you criticize Norm Hill."

I delivered a speech before Mr. W. Clement Stone's managers down in Miami, Florida about six years ago in which I described for them, as I have described for you, my ten invisible guides. When I got down to Norm Hill, you should have heard these men laugh. They thought it was terribly funny. But within six months, every one of those men was using the same plan, and not only were they using it in connection with getting such minor things as parking spots, but they were also sending their salesmen out. Their salesmen work under what is called "cold turkey"—that is to say, everybody they meet is a prospect. They don't have to have an appointment. Those salesmen were using that same plan, and they were sending Norm Hill ahead to talk to the man they were going to interview and selling him before the salesman ever got on the job. Is that an astounding thing?

When these men first started that plan, Mr. Stone's men were earning, I should say, an average of $175–$200 a week, and within a year after that, they were averaging around $250–$500 a week, entirely because Norm Hill had changed their mental attitudes so that when they went in to sell the man they didn't hear him when he said, "No." They kept on talking. Is that an astounding thing?

Most of us here know what's coming before the man says it. We know he's going to say "no," and he picks up our mental attitude and reflects it back to us as his own. I used to work in a bank when I was a youngster as a teller. And I could tell when a man came into the front door and started toward my cage whether he expected to get what he was coming after or not. I certainly could. I could tell it every time by the way he walked, by the way he looked around furtively, and by his attempt to engage me in useless conversation after he got up to the teller's cage before he presented the check—all intended to throw me off balance. An astounding thing what you can do dealing with people if you understand these principles that I'm now talking about.

We've just about conquered everything in the universe; we're now trying to conquer outer space. We've about done everything we can to uncover the powers of nature, but there's one yet unresolved objective we have not attained. We haven't learned how to live with one another. One of the greatest things that this philosophy can do for you and those whom you contact and the world around you is to teach people how to live with one another under the master mind principle so that they have more joy in living, they have more prosperity, they have better health, and they make this a better country in which to live.

I thank you. Thank you. Thank you.

Chapter 3

Applied Faith

Dr. Hill: Applied faith is a wonderful subject, and if there's one man in the whole world that ought to know about it, I am perhaps that one man because I've had opportunities for the last fifty years to test this principle in almost every circumstance of life. Actually, my whole lecture is based on this statement: Whatever the mind of man can conceive and believe, it can achieve.

I think probably one of the most outstanding illustrations of what the power of faith can do is connected with the birth of my second son, Blair. When Blair came into the world, he came without any ears. He had no sign of ears. The two doctors, who were his mother's uncles who brought him into the world, met me out in the rotunda of the hospital hoping to soften the shock that I would undergo when I saw my son. They explained the condition under which he was born. They explained that there had been a few other children known to medical science born under similar circumstances, but they wanted me to know in advance that not one of them ever learned to hear or to speak, and they wanted me to know also that I should prepare myself to go through life with a son who would be a deaf mute. Well, that's as far as they got. I stopped them right there. I said, "Now listen, doctors, I haven't seen my son but I can tell you this: He'll not be a deaf mute and he'll go through life with 100 percent of his hearing just like all normal children."

One of these doctors, who hadn't been doing the talking, came over and put his hands on my shoulder. He said, "Now look here, Napoleon, there are some things in this world that neither you nor I nor anyone else can do anything about, and you might just as well recognize now that you face one of those circumstances."

I said, "Doctor, there isn't anything in this world that I can't do something about. If it's nothing more than adjust myself to an unpleasant circumstance, so that it doesn't break my heart, I can do that." I started immediately to do just that. I made up my mind before I saw my son that under no circumstances was I going to accept him as a deaf mute. Under no circumstances was I going to accept his condition as an affliction. Under no circumstances was I going to stop until he had 100 percent of his hearing. I had no idea how it was going to come about. The only thing that I was sure about was that it was going to come about. And I want to tell you that when you go at anything with that attitude, you're using applied faith.

I went to work on my child before I ever saw him, with prayer. For the next four years, I spent at least four hours a day working on him, communicating with him through his subconscious mind, and up to the eighteenth month, we knew positively that nothing happened. But that didn't destroy my faith; I knew something would happen. We kept on working on him. We gave him every test available as to his hearing, and he wasn't hearing anything up to eighteen months. Then a strange thing happened. We knew that he was hearing. We didn't know how much he was hearing, but I could snap my fingers; I remember he turned to see which way the noise came from, and we knew he was hearing. By the time he was four years of age, we had developed 65 percent of his normal hearing through my prayers and my communications to his subconscious mind. Which of the two did the most good I don't know; maybe it was the combination of the two.

This 65 percent of his normal hearing was enough to get him to the primary school, through high school, and to the third year in college. During the third year in college, the Acousticon company, which makes hearing aids, heard about this unusual case, the only one of its kind in the world where a child born without ears ever learned to hear or to speak. They came down to the University of West Virginia at Morgantown and made my son a special hearing aid that gave him the other 35 percent of his normal hearing, and today he has 100 percent of his normal hearing just like I said he would have. Doctors came from all over the world. They made hundreds and hundreds of x-rays of his brain after they found out that 65 percent of his normal hearing had been developed. They wanted to find out if they could find any physical organ through which he was hearing, and they never found any; they never did. Another queer thing about it is that Blair can hear just as well with his hearing aid on his spine back here as he can with it on his head—just as well.

Dr. Irving Voorhees was a distinguished ear specialist in New York who had the privilege of examining Blair. I asked Dr. Voorhees what he thought had happened that enabled this child to hear. "Well," he said, "undoubtedly it was the process that you went through in dealing with him, whatever it was; undoubted, that's what happened. If you hadn't done that, he undoubtedly would have been a deaf mute just like all the other children who have been born under the same circumstances." Blair today has 100 percent of his hearing. He's a successful and prosperous businessman. He's getting joy out of life.

From the very beginning, I taught him that the condition under which he was born was no affliction at all. It was a great blessing because people who had observed the condition he was in would go out of their way to be nice to him, and that's exactly what happened. It was a great blessing, ladies and gentlemen, not only in that one way but in many ways. It was a great blessing because it enabled me to learn about the power of prayer as I never would have learned from any other source. There are a lot of people who give lip service to prayer, but that's just about all. I gave more than lip service. I threw my heart and soul into this child and I made up my mind, if there was any first cause, if there was any God, I was going to get through to him and I was going to get a response, and I got through, and I got the response. If you think that that doesn't take courage, if you think that doesn't draw upon your sources of faith, it's because you haven't ever experienced what I have experienced. I've often thought what a great blessing it was that God sent me a son without any ears in order to let me prove to myself there was no such thing as impossibility, that prayer can do anything and everything.

While I was advertising manager of the LaSalle Extension University many years ago, I happened to meet a clergyman by the name of Reverend Frank W. Gunsaulus. Dr. Gunsaulus had a little church out in the stockyard section of Chicago and a little bit of a following—not very much—and I imagine they weren't much more than paying him enough to live on. But he had a multimillion dollar idea. He had long wanted to start a new type of school—a technical school where students would study book learning, so to speak, half of the day, and they'd go into the laboratory or into an industrial plant and apply what they learned the other half.

When he made up his budget, he found that he had to have a million dollars in order to get the thing off the ground to start with, but he didn't have a million dollars. He thought of this for four or five years, procrastinated on it. Then he did something unusual. Without ever having heard of the Science of Personal Achievement or of Napoleon Hill, he commenced to use Definiteness of Purpose. He got up one morning and he said, "I am going to raise a million dollars, I'm going to do it within one week, and I'm going to do it myself, alone." He wrote a sermon entitled "What I Would Do if I Had a Million Dollars" and announced in the Chicago Tribune that he would preach on that subject the next Sunday.

He wrote out this speech word for word, rehearsed it, and went over it, and on the Sunday morning when he was to deliver the sermon, before he went to his church, he knelt down on the floor at his home and prayed for one hour that someone who had a million dollars would see that announcement in the Chicago Tribune and would hear his sermon and would supply the million dollars for him. When he was sure that his prayer had gotten across, he jumped up and ran. When he got into his church two miles away, he reached into his pocket for his notes as he went into his pulpit and, lo and behold, they weren't there—he'd left them on the floor at home. He said, "Well, Lord, it's up to you and me. I've done all I can do, and Lord, I hope that you'll help me out because if I ever needed you, I need you now."

I talked to some of his parishioners years later, and they said that he went into that pulpit and delivered a sermon the likes of which they had never heard before and never heard afterward. He told the audience what he would do if he had a million dollars, why he needed it, and how it would change the lives of people. He outlined his plan, and when he finished, a stranger who was sitting in the last row got up and walked slowly down the aisle and reached up and took Dr. Gunsaulus's hand and pulled him over and whispered for a few moments in his ear and then walked back and sat down. Dr. Gunsaulus said, "My friends, you have just witnessed a miracle. The gentleman who just walked down the aisle and shook hands with me is Philip D. Armour, and he says if I will come down to his office, he will arrange for me to have the million dollars." And that's how Dr. Gunsaulus got the first million dollars to start the Armour Institute of Technology in Chicago, which, in recent years, has been consolidated with the University of Illinois.

A preacher raising a million dollars in one week because he became definite! He believed in what he was doing; he knew it was right that he should have the million dollars, and he laid out a plan and moved on it. The trouble with most of us is that when we lay out a plan, we sleep on it, we procrastinate over it, and we dream about it, but we don't get into action, and that's not applied faith. If you don't do something that poses a risk in connection with your faith, it's not applied faith—it's just the faith of good intentions. You've got to back faith with action, and that's just what most people don't do.

Here is another experience I had a good many years ago: I was lecturing in Milwaukee, Wisconsin, and I noticed a couple of young men bringing in an old gentleman on a cot. They brought him right down in front where I was speaking and propped him up. I noticed that all the way through my talk he never batted an eye, he never moved a hand, he didn't do anything; he just laid there. I was so curious that when I was through speaking, I went down and introduced myself to the young men and found out they were his sons and that he was Milo C. Jones, a farmer from Fort Atkinson, Wisconsin, and I heard his story—a most astounding story.

He had 160 acres of land on which he and his family were just barely making a living, and he had the bad fortune to undergo a stroke resulting in double paralysis. Absolutely all his muscles were destroyed. He couldn't move a hand, he couldn't move a leg, he couldn't move a foot. He could talk after a fashion. That is to say, he could mutter so that his family could understand what he was saying. After the stroke, they rolled him out on the front porch in the wheelchair while the rest of the family went about doing the farm work, and that went on for about three weeks. Then Milo C. Jones made a great discovery, a discovery which the majority of people in the whole realm of mankind never discovers. He discovered that he had a mind and that that mind was incapable of being stopped from attaining anything it wanted, that mind had been left intact, and it had not been paralyzed. He started to work with his mind, and in a matter of days it came up with an idea. He called his family around him and said, "I want you to start immediately to planting every acre of ground that we have in corn."

One of the boys said, "But Father, we can't do that. We've got to save some of it for pasturage."

"No," he said, "plant every acre of it in corn and start feeding that corn to young pigs, and while they're still young, slaughter them and make them into little pig sausage." And ladies and gentlemen, long before Milo C. Jones died some ten years later, he became a multimillionaire on the same 160 acres where he was previously just making a living. Isn't that an astounding thing, what real faith can do? A perfectly astounding thing.

I had an interesting experiment in the commercial field with my former manager, Mr. W. Clement Stone, five or six years ago. Mr. Stone's estate is near to the campus of Northwestern University, and he became acquainted with a number of the professors over at the University. One of the professors came over to Mr. Stone's house one evening and said, "I've been over at Northwestern University quite a while. I'm just about making a living, and I have some young children coming along, so I decided that I had to do something about it to make a better income, and I went into the insurance business. I've got a job now with an insurance company. I'm going to sell insurance, and I just wondered— knowing how successful you are in the insurance business—if you would mind giving me the names of ten or fifteen people as prospects who I may call on and use your name."

"Why," Mr. Stone said, "I'll be delighted to do that. If you'll come down to the office tomorrow morning, I'll have my secretary make them out and have them all neatly fixed on cards for you."

When he went down next morning, Mr. Stone called him in and gave him the cards, and the fellow said, "Now, Mister Stone, is it all right for me to use your name?"

Mr. Stone said, "Exactly right. You can just tell them it was at my request that you're calling on them."

He went to work, and before the end of the week, he came running back and said, "Mister Stone, Mister Stone, I've sold eight out of the ten and I've got appointments with the other two, and won't you make me out ten more cards?"

Mr. Stone said, "You hit me at a bad time. I'm busy right now, but here's the telephone book. You can copy them out of there; that's where I got them."

The man said, "No, you didn't."

And Mr. Stone said, "Yes, I started with the As. I got one out of the As, one out of the Bs, one out of the Cs, one out of the Ds, and right on down to ten cards, and you can do the same thing. You can copy them just as well as I can."

This man was so shocked, he couldn't believe what Mr. Stone said, but Mr. Stone finally convinced him that that's exactly where he got them. He said, "Now, you sit down and make up ten cards." And he did—made up ten cards and went out and worked a whole week and didn't get an interview except on two occasions, let alone make a sale. So, what happened there? Was it the fault of the prospects that he didn't get an interview and didn't make a sale? No, they had nothing to do with it. The fault was up here in the man's head. He didn't believe he could make a sale. He didn't believe you could take a name out of a telephone book and go out cold turkey, so to speak, get an interview, and make a sale. He didn't believe that. But when Mr. Stone gave him ten cards where he could say, "Mister Stone sent me," he thought that had a great influence with the prospective buyer. It probably had no influence whatever, but the mental attitude of the man doing the talking did have an influence on the prospective buyers.

I have trained over thirty thousand salesmen, and one of the most important things that I have taught every one of them (and which I hope to get across to you, ladies and gentlemen) is that no one ever makes a sale to anybody of anything at any time without having first made the sale to himself.

You study any great leader or any great salesman or any great lawyer or any great clergyman, any great anybody whose business it is to influence people, and you'll find out that the ones who do the best job are the ones who have sold themselves lock, stock, and barrel on what they're going to do or say. The reason Billy Graham gets a big crowd and holds them and does a better job than any thousand ordinary clergymen that you could pick out is that he's got a better attitude about what he's doing. He just knows that what he's doing is right. You know the lawyer who doesn't believe in the merits of his client seldom wins any cases. And the clergyman who doesn't believe in the statements made in his sermon very seldom makes any converts. It's this matter of belief that really counts. It's the most mysterious, the most marvelous, and the most powerful thing in the universe—the capacity to believe.

Another thing I have noticed about these great leaders is that they have the capacity to hypnotize themselves into believing that they can do whatever they want to do. Self-hypnosis. Whether you're afraid of that term or not is beside the point. You're indulging in it every minute of the day whether you know it or not. We all are. That man who has risen to great heights, no better educated, no brighter, no more intelligent than the man who has not, has learned how to condition his own mind to believe that whatever he wants to do, he can and will do.

I was called in by the superintendent of the New York Life Insurance Company some years ago, and he said, "Mister Hill, we have a salesman here who, up until a couple of years ago, led every man on the staff, and now he's gone sour and he's thinking about quitting. His sales have dropped down to where they amount to practically nothing. We want to know if you wouldn't analyze him and find out what the trouble is."

I said, "I'll be very glad to." They brought him in. His name was James C. Spring, sixty-five years young. I talked to Mr. Spring for a little while, and I soon found out what happened. His wife made the mistake one day of referring to him as "the old man," and suddenly he became an old man, too old to sell. I said, "Mister Spring, I'd like to have you go out on calls—do you have some prospects?" "Oh," he says, "I have a pocketful of them." I said, "All right, tomorrow morning we start. You pick out ten, and we'll call on them tomorrow or in the next two days, and I'll go along and listen. I won't say a word, but I want to hear you put on your pitch. Then I'll comment on your sales talk."

I could tell before we approached the first prospect that he was afraid that the man was not going to buy; I could just feel it. His fear was exuding out and penetrating his whole makeup. And sure enough, the man turned him down. The next one wouldn't even see him. That went on, and he didn't make a sale and didn't get but two interviews out of the ten.

I knew then what had to be done. We went back to the agency and I said, "Now I know what's wrong with Mister Spring, and I'm going to tell him what the remedy is. He hears the word 'no' before he even sees the man he's going to sell to. Before he goes in, he knows the man's going to say 'no,' and by golly, generally, he does because the man picks up out of Spring's mind exactly what Spring's thinking about. And that happens in every case where two people come together as prospect and salesman."

"Mister Spring," said I, "I want you to go out here in some of these pawn shops and get one of those old fashioned ear trumpets. I want one that's banged up, showing that you've been using it a long time. I don't want a new one."

"Just what the heck do you want with that?" I said, "That's my business. You go out and get it and do just like I said, and we're going out over that same list of prospects we went over last week. And when a man says 'no,' I want you to put that trumpet right up to your ear and make out like you didn't hear him and go right on talking."

You know what happened? Mr. Spring got back on the beam, and he excelled his previous record. He was ready to retire, but for the next six years he led everybody in the New York division of the New York Life Insurance Company. Isn't that an astounding thing, what a little psychology can do to change the mental attitude of a man from fear to applied faith?

You've got to learn to work some tricks on yourself too. The subconscious mind doesn't know the difference between a penny and a million dollars. It does not know the difference between success and failure, and it'll work just as hard to make a failure out of you as it will to make a success out of you if you don't condition your mind to keep the subconscious mind working with and for the things you want and away from the things you don't want. The majority of people spend the majority of their lives worrying and fearing and fretting over the things they don't want, and that's exactly what they're getting out of life.

I try to make allowances for the weaknesses and for the mistakes of other people that affect my interest. I don't always do a good job of it, but I try. I try to keep my mental attitude positive at all times toward all people about all subjects. I want to tell you that this effort on my part has gone a long way toward placing me in a position where I can say, as I said to you this morning, that I have acquired in this life everything that I need, everything that I want, everything that I desire. I have no fears, no frustrations, and no disappointments. I have good, sound health. I have a happy home.

Thank you very much. Next time we will talk about the characteristics of a pleasing personality and the importance of going the extra mile.

Chapter 4

Pleasing Personality
and Going the Extra Mile

Dr. Hill: Here are some of the more important traits of a pleasing personality: First of all, a positive mental attitude, based upon one's expression by words or thoughts or deeds or the emotions, among which the most important emotions are positive emotions (faith, hope, love, enthusiasm, sex, loyalty, and cheerfulness) and negative emotions (fear). The seven basic fears are fear of poverty, fear of ill health, fear of criticism, fear of the loss of love of someone, fear of the loss of liberty, fear of old age, and fear of death.

Second, flexibility. That is to say, the ability to unbend mentally and physically and to adapt oneself to any circumstance or environment without loss of self-control or composure. Flexibility is a trait of the extrovert, a person who can and does take a keen interest in and expresses himself on behalf of other people. The flexible person has full control of his emotions at all times.

Then, pleasing tone of voice—that is, a voice controlled and cultivated to express any desired feeling and free from sharp nasal tones that indicate a fault-finding attitude.

And frankness of manner and speech but with discriminant control of the tongue at all times, based upon the habit of thinking before speaking.

And a keen sense of justice toward all people and applied in all human relationships, even when to do so may appear unprofitable.

Sincerity of purpose in all human relationships, remembering that insincerity begets failure of friendly cooperation.

Tactfulness of speech and manner, remembering that not all thoughts should be expressed even though one may speak the truth.

Promptness of decision when all of the facts for a decision are available.

Faith in infinite intelligence, based on observation of the orderliness of the universe, the visible portions of the world, and the universe at large.

Controlled enthusiasm—that is to say, the ability to turn on and off one's interest at will, with a special attention to enthusiasm in speech.

Common courtesy, both in speech and in mental attitude. I know of no one quality of a pleasing personality that pays off so handsomely as that of ordinary courtesy.

And then the habit of going the extra mile—that is to say, rendering more service and better service than one is paid to do and doing it all the time.

Those are some of the most important traits of a pleasing personality.

Narrator: *You have just heard Dr. Hill give the highlights of the thirty traits of a pleasing personality. Now we ask that for the next few moments you grade yourself on each of these traits. We will allow you time to answer to yourself. May we recommend that you answer excellent, good, or restudy. And we're sure that you will quickly recognize those traits that do need improving. Here are Napoleon Hill's thirty traits of a pleasing personality:*

1. *A positive mental attitude*
2. *Flexibility*
3. *Sincerity of purpose*
4. *Promptness of decision*
5. *Courtesy on all occasions*
6. *Pleasant tone of voice*
7. *Habit of smiling when speaking*
8. *Pleasant facial expression*
9. *Tactfulness in speech*
10. *Tolerance with all people*
11. *Frankness in manner and speech*
12. *A keen sense of humor*
13. *Faith in infinite intelligence*
14. *A keen sense of justice*
15. *Appropriateness of words*
16. *Control of emotional feelings*
17. *Alertness of interest*
18. *Effective speech*
19. *Versatility in general*

20. *Fondness for people*

21. *Control of temper at will*

22. *Hope and ambition for success*

23. *Temperance in all habits*

24. *Patience*

25. *Humility of the heart*

26. *Appropriateness of clothing*

27. *Good showmanship*

28. *Clean sportsmanship*

29. *Ability to shake hands gracefully*

30. *Personal magnetism*

Our next principle provides an unfailing rule for making others recognize one's outstanding abilities. Dr. Hill, how would you define this important principle, going the extra mile?

Dr. Hill: It means rendering more service and better service than you are paid to render and doing it all the time and doing it in a pleasing, positive mental attitude. Let me relate my experience with Franklin D. Roosevelt in the White House in 1933—it will give you a fine indication of how the students of this philosophy may profit by this important principle.

When I went to work for the President in 1933, nothing was said at the beginning about how much I was to receive or who was to pay it. I had been there about three months when one day, Franklin D. Roosevelt asked me who was paying my salary and how much I was getting. I said, "Well, Mister President, that's something I would like to know myself. I haven't heard anything about it." We talked on for a little while and I said, "Mister

President, you know I have been serving you ever since you were Assistant Secretary of the Navy and particularly while you were Governor of New York, and you will recall, of course, that up to this time I have never rendered you a bill or asked you to pay me a dollar for my services, and I'm not going to start now, but if you insist upon it, suppose you put me on the payroll at a dollar a year." And that's exactly what he did.

I took my typewriter down to the White House, and when I wasn't actually serving the President or some member of his staff or cabinet, I started writing books. I wrote six books that first year, among them *Think and Grow Rich*, the book that has made me popular all over the world, you might say. I had no intention of publishing that book when I was writing it; I was writing it to myself to keep my mind positive in those days of chaos. Some three years after I left the service of the President, I got out these manuscripts and read them, and I made up my mind that the only one worth publishing was *Think and Grow Rich*. When I took it to my publisher, he said, "What is in this book that leads you to believe it would sell?"

I said, "You will have to read it to find out."

He took it home with him and read it. He had his whole staff read it paragraph by paragraph, and then they took a vote on it, and they voted unanimously that it was the best manuscript that ever came to that publishing house. They printed it and put it to work, and it's been selling as a best seller all over the world up to this time. It has grossed over eighteen million dollars and probably will gross many more millions of dollars while I'm still alive. I think if you will stop and consider the wages that I asked, the wages I received of one dollar a year and the service that I gave for that, you'll recognize what can be accomplished by going the extra mile.

Now let me give you some of the benefits that come from going the extra mile. It places the law of increasing returns square back of one. It brings one to the favorable attention of those who can and do provide opportunities for promotion. It tends to permit one to become indispensable in many different human relationships and therefore enables one to command more than average compensation. It leads to a mental growth and physical perfection in various forms of service, thereby developing greater ability and skill in one's chosen vocation. It protects one against the loss of employment and places one in a position to choose his own job and working conditions. It enables one to profit by the law of contrast because the majority of people do not practice the habit of going the extra mile. As a matter of fact, the majority of people don't even go the first mile. It leads to the development of a positive mental attitude, which is among the more important traits of a pleasing personality. And it tends to develop a keen alert imagination, as it is a habit which keeps one continuously seeking new and more efficient ways of rendering service. It definitely serves to develop self-reliance. It serves also to build the confidence of others in one's integrity. And it is the only logical reason to justify one in asking for a promotion or for more wages because if a man is not doing any more than he's paid for, then obviously he has no right to ask for more pay.

With these facts, you can understand why I place so much importance on this principle. It has been called "the best plan for raising your own salary." Search wherever you will for a single sound argument against this principle and you will not find it, nor will you find a single instance of enduring success which was not attained in part by its application. The principle is not the creation of man; it is a part of nature's handiwork. For it is obvious that every living creature below the intelligence of man is forced to apply the principle in order to survive. Man may disregard the principle if he chooses, but he cannot do so and at the same time enjoy the fruits of enduring success.

There is much to be said for the old cliché "service with a smile." If your attitude outwardly and inwardly is positive and you go the extra mile, giving extra service over and above that prescribed by your job description, then you are well on your way to worthwhile relationships that can not only be pleasant but often splendidly rewarding in speeding you toward the achievement of your highest goals.

The habit of giving more and better service than you are paid for brings rewards in many forms. It will attract the favorable attention of the right people who will provide you with opportunities for self-advancement. Very often the returns will come from an entirely unexpected source, not from the person you enthusiastically help. The law of increasing returns will go to work for you. The extra seeds of service you sow will come back to you greatly multiplied in one form or another. The more we give, the more we get. Bread cast upon the water will return to sustain and to strengthen the man who is rendering more service and better service than he is paid or expected to do. Returns do not always come from the person to whom the gift or service was given. They often do not, in fact. But returns will come. They may be early or they may be late, but they will come. The gifts, the words, the attitudes, the withholding of the gifts, the withholding of the words, and what you do and are will come home.

What is it you seek? Self-satisfaction? Revenge? Help another to experience these things and they will become your own. Is it wealth? A superior grasp of some secrets of success? Is it more effective efforts towards business expansion? The entire history of mankind, from the Stone Age to the present, provides indisputable evidence that man's only real limitations are those which he sets up in his own mind or accepts in the circumstances which surround him. Fear will make a man miserly of his money, of his time, of his talents, and of his inner resources. Examine this thought: A man may give more time than is called for out of fear, but the time will be given reluctantly and without real productiveness. His body may be weary, but he is resentfully weary, and sleep will not come easily as it does after physical strain willingly exerted.

But consider the man who goes the extra mile because he is eager to help get the job done well. Willingness to work extra hours and to do the extra bit of effort that puts the polish on an adequate product results in a rewarding flood of well-being in the innermost consciousness. Even if no one notices at that moment or says "thank you," it is enough to know that one has done a good job, an extra good job, and that the pay is earned. The pure joy of having done more and a better job than was expected is what makes the difference between a worker and a drone. It is the difference between a period and an exclamation point.

Going the extra mile pays off in prosperity, both in the heart and in the pocketbook, but do not forget that it is a fragile phenomenon. It must be tempered with self-discipline as a reminder that the gift is not primarily to get a gift in return but is a mile given, an hour of overtime expended willingly, with the foremost idea being to help thy brother's boat to shore. If you can perfect the attitude of helpfulness for the pure joy of doing a better job for another person, then the delicate balance will become a part of your nature with unexpected dividends being realized in your own life.

Chapter 5

Personal Initiative and Self-Discipline

Narrator: *We are now at the sixth principle in our Science of Personal Achievement: personal initiative. Personal initiative is the principle necessary for leadership in any walk of life. Dr. Hill, wasn't this a trait possessed by virtually all of your five hundred collaborators in the development of this success philosophy?*

Dr. Hill: It was an outstanding trait in every one of them. Not a single one of the five hundred men who helped me to build the Science of Personal Achievement was without the active application of this habit of moving on his own personal initiative. Let me give you illustrations of some of the outstanding men who have attained great success by applying this principle, along with the other sixteen principles of the philosophy.

Take Henry J. Kaiser, for instance. During World War II, he was in the business of building ships for the government, and he needed special cars of material to be shipped in, and this material had to be delivered absolutely on time. He didn't take any chances. In order to make sure that the material would come through on time, he put two expeditors on every train carrying material—one to stay awake all the time while the other one slept—and they rode those cars straight across the continent, and they were given instructions that if any railroad man dared to sidetrack those cars, they should get the president of the railroad company on the telephone immediately and demand that those cars move. That's how definitely Mr. Kaiser moved in seeing that his personal initiative was carried out.

Take the great American way of life. It's based on the principle of personal initiative. It's carried out by its leaders in industry. The application of the principle of following through dates back to the days of the American Revolution when those determined men signed the Declaration of Independence, one of the greatest documents known to mankind. It took definiteness of purpose for them to do that. And take Orville and Wilbur Wright, for instance, in the development of the airplane. I had the privilege of riding with Orville Wright in the first airplane that the Wright brothers built. They were demonstrating the possibility of the plane's successful flying to the Navy in Washington, and they chose me as a passenger to ride from Washington down to Alexandria and back—ten miles. That demonstration made it possible for the Navy to buy one plane. Before Orville and Wilbur Wright succeeded in developing this airplane, they failed many times, but they went on, on their own personal initiative.

And take Thomas A. Edison and the development of the incandescent electric lamp. Imagine a man, for instance, standing by through ten thousand different failures as Mr. Edison did without giving up. His personal initiative was so definite that he told me that if he hadn't found the secret of the incandescent electric lamp that at that very moment he would be in the laboratory working on it instead of being out there wasting his time talking with me. Then on a more serious note, Mr. Edison said, "You know I had to succeed because I finally ran out of things that wouldn't work." I've thought of that so many times, wondering why more people don't keep on keeping on until they run out of things that won't work for them; they're bound to find the thing that will work.

And take myself, for example, in devoting more than twenty years to research for the missing link of this philosophy, now known as the law of cosmic habit force. My persistent personal initiative finally yielded a full and workable description of this great law of nature into which all the other sixteen principles of this philosophy blend and on which they must depend for automatic application.

To be fully realized, the habit of personal initiative must begin by its application in the small unimportant circumstances of one's daily life. For example, it is the antidote for procrastination. It is the beginning of all big and small achievements.

Narrator: *I have heard you say, Dr. Hill, that there are many starters among men today but there are few finishers. How will an application of this lesson remedy that situation?*

Dr. Hill: It will remedy it by the student's forming the habit of moving on his own personal initiative in connection with everything he does and standing by this habit, never putting off until tomorrow the thing that should be done today or maybe the day before yesterday. In other words, he should adopt the motto "Do it now" and then stand by that motto.

There are many starters among men today but there are few finishers. The most common cause for failure is the habit of drifting through life without a definite major purpose. You must develop the habit of personal initiative if your plans are to lead to success. It has been said that personal initiative bears the same relationship to an individual that a self-starter bears to an automobile. Personal initiative, to be effective as a quality of leadership, must be based upon a definite organized plan inspired by a definite motive and followed through to the end at which it is aimed.

The big four results of personal initiative are:

1. It ensures one to choose a definite major purpose and to follow through with a definite plan of action for the attainment of that purpose

2. It gives springs of action to the habit of going the extra mile

3. It inspires the organization of a master mind alliance

4. It clears the mind for guidance through applied faith

Five of the major attributes which are essential for leadership are:

1. Personal initiative

2. The adoption of a definite major purpose

3. An adequate motive to inspire continuous action in pursuit of the object of a definite major purpose

4. A master mind alliance through which the power essential for the attainment of a definite major purpose may be acquired

5. Self-reliance in proportion to the scope and object of one's major purpose

Personal initiative is a trait much admired and, if carried out with discretion and logic, can very quickly put you ahead of the crowd. Initiative built on a definite understanding of what must be achieved puts one in harmony with everyone around him and with the universe as a whole. If one has a definite goal in mind, then opportunities for personal initiative are easy to find. Initiative is the first step. It is an indication of a good attitude displayed through action. It is the self-reliant demonstration which seldom goes unnoticed by those in authority. Personal initiative is self confidence in action, and if you are moving toward a definite goal, it speeds your journey and smooths the way for good work to become easier and more rewarding.

Narrator: *We now begin our discussion of the 7th principle, self-discipline, with this rather profound statement by Napoleon Hill: "There is no single requirement for individual success as important as self-discipline." That statement could step on a lot of people's toes, Dr. Hill, but you magnificently show how important it is for us to control our thoughts and our emotions. In this regard, could you comment on the importance of a person taking complete possession of his or her own mind?*

Dr. Hill: Yes. The power of thought is the only thing over which you have complete, unchallenged, and unchallengeable control—control by power of will. In giving human beings control over but one thing, the Creator must have chosen the most important of all things. This is a stupendous fact that merits your most profound consideration. If you give it this sort of consideration, you will discover for yourself the rich promises available to those who become masters of their own mind power, who employ self-discipline. Self-discipline leads to sound physical health, and it leads to peace of mind, development of harmony within one's own mind. It enables one to keep the mind fixed upon that which is wanted and off of that which is not wanted.

The majority of people go all the way through life with most of their mind power fixed upon their fears and their discouragements and things they don't want. You will have acquired sufficient self-discipline to enable you to find health, wealth, and happiness when you can close the door of your mind to all the things you do not want, for then and then only will the door to all the things you do want open to you. The past is gone forever; close the door of your mind against it, and lo, the door to a hopeful future will open in front of you. The failure, defeat, illness, disappointment, and fears of the past have no place as controlling factors in your life. Close the door against them all—close it tight. Close it good and tight, and you will have gained a victory in self-discipline that will be priceless to you throughout life.

Narrator: *The late Mahatma Gandhi, who introduced all of your writings to India, was, I believe, your number one student insofar as the application of this lesson on self-discipline is concerned.*

Dr. Hill: Yes, he was. Just think of that one man defeating the entire military forces of the British government, freeing his people, and sending the British military forces home without the firing of a gun or the killing of a soldier. That's a stupendous illustration of what the mind can accomplish.

Self-discipline is attained by the control of thought habits, and the term "self-discipline" has reference only to the power of thought because all discipline of self must take place in the mind, although its effects may deal with the functions of the physical body. You are where you are and what you are because of your habits of thought. Your thought habits are subject to your control. They are the only circumstances of your life over which you have complete control, which is the most profound of all the facts of your life because it clearly proves that your Creator recognized the necessity of this great prerogative. Otherwise, he would not have made it the sole circumstance over which man has been given exclusive control. Further evidence of the Creator's desire to give man the unchallengeable right of control over his thought habits has been clearly revealed through the law of cosmic habit force, the medium by which thought habits are fixed and made permanent so that habits become automatic and operate without the voluntary effort of man.

For the present, we are interested only in calling attention to the fact that the Creator of the marvelous mechanism known as the brain ingeniously provided it with a device by which all thought habits are taken over and given automatic expression. Self-discipline is the principle by which one may voluntarily shape the patterns of thought to harmonize with one's aims and purposes. This privilege carries with it a heavy responsibility because it is the one privilege which determines, more than all others, the position in life which each man shall occupy. If this privilege is neglected by one's failure to voluntarily form habits designed to lead to the attainment of definite ends, then the circumstances of life which are beyond one's control will do the job, and what an extremely poor job they will do. Every man is a bundle of habits. Some are of his own making while others are involuntary. They are made by his fears and doubts, his worries and anxieties, his greed and superstitions, and his envy and hatred.

The man who is not the master of himself may never become the master of anything. He who is the master of self may become the master of his own earthly destiny, the master of his fate, the captain of his soul. The highest form of self-discipline consists in the expression of humility of the heart when one has attained great riches or has been overtaken by that which is commonly called success.

Self-discipline is the only means by which one's habits of thought may be controlled and directed until they are taken over and given automatic expression by the law of cosmic habit force. Ponder this carefully, for it is the key to your mental, physical, and spiritual destiny. Let me repeat: Self-discipline is the only means by which one's habits of thought may be controlled and directed until they are taken over and given automatic expression by the law of cosmic habit force. You can make your thought habits to order, and they will carry you to the attainment of any desired goal within your reach, or you can allow the uncontrollable circumstances of your life to make your thought habits for you, and they'll carry you irresistibly into the failure side of the great river of life. You can keep your mind trained on that which you desire from life and get just that, or you can feed it on thoughts of that which you do not desire, and it will as unerringly bring you just that. Your thought habits evolve from the food that your mind dwells upon; that is as certain as that night follows day.

Awake, arise, and quicken your mind to the attunement of the circumstances of life which your heart craves. Turn on the full powers of your will, and take complete control of your own mind. It is your mind. It was given to you as a servant to carry out your desires, and no one may enter it or influence it in the slightest degree without your consent and cooperation. What a profound fact that is. Remember this when the circumstances over which you appear to have no control begin to move in and aggravate you. Remember it when fear and doubt and worry begin to park themselves in the spare bedroom of your mind. Remember it when the fear of poverty begins to park itself in the space of your mind that should be filled with a prosperity consciousness. And remember, too, that this is self-discipline: the one and only method by which anyone may take full possession of his own mind.

You are not a worm made to crawl in the dust of the earth. If you were, you would have been equipped with the physical means by which you could have crawled on your belly instead of walking on your two legs. Your physical body was designed to enable you to stand and to walk and to think your way to the highest attainment which you are capable of conceiving. Why be contented with less? Why should you insult your Creator by indifference or neglect in the use of his most priceless gift—the power of your own mind?

Self-discipline is training which corrects, molds, strengthens, and perfects. Your behavior and your attitudes are expressions of your thoughts. Much of our thinking seems to be uncontrolled, random thinking or is on a semiconscious level. From time to time, we are aware of our feelings. Feelings may indicate that we have been thinking strongly on certain subjects. When we feel, we become more alert because we have become aware of power and energy stimulated by thought. We may be stimulated to love, faith, and loyalty, or to fear, jealousy, greed, and anger. Self-discipline teaches us to direct the energy generated by our thoughts into feeling and action that will be advantageous and strengthening. Self-discipline will help direct our energy into the most useful successful channels.

Chapter 6

Controlled Attention and Enthusiasm

Narrator: *Controlled attention is the act of coordinating all the faculties of the mind and directing their combined power to a given end. Dr. Hill, why is it so important to concentrate on one's major purpose?*

Dr. Hill: The main reason for concentrating upon a major purpose is that if you don't do that, you dissipate your mind power by allowing it to dwell on relatively unimportant things. The men of great achievement have all learned the art of concentrating upon one definite major purpose in life. Of course they have other minor purposes, but I'm talking now about a major overall purpose. Let us take a look at some of them.

Henry Ford's major purpose, for instance, was his desire to build a low-priced automobile, and while he was chided by his relatives and by the public at large for wasting his time on that "contraption," as they called it, Ford was the first man in the entire world to build automobiles successfully. He concentrated his mind on that and didn't allow it to be diverted to anything else.

Thomas A. Edison's controlled attention was directed toward invention, and he became the most outstanding inventor of all times, as you of course know.

Mine, for instance, is concentration upon the philosophy of personal achievement, and I have now devoted fifty-five years to doing just that, with the result that I have reached the minds of millions of people in practically all of the free countries of the world. Before I pass on, I hope to see the philosophy introduced to all of the nations of the world.

John D. Rockefeller's major purpose was to concentrate upon the producing and the refining and the marketing of oil, and he made a stupendous fortune out of it. Ralph Waldo Emerson's act of concentration was probing the depths of men's thoughts and thinking processes. F. W. Woolworth's concentration was directed to the building and the operation of five and ten cent stores, and as a result of his concentrating upon that one source of merchandising, he made himself a multimillionaire, and at the time of his death he had built the tallest building in the United States, the Woolworth Building in New York.

William Wrigley Jr.'s act of concentration was directed to the manufacturing of a package of chewing gum, a five cent package of chewing gum, and he also built a tremendous fortune out of that small item of merchandising. Incidentally, Mr. William Wrigley was the first student of this philosophy that I had. Back in the early days, he and five of his associates became students of this philosophy, and they paid me the first money that I ever received for teaching it. I remember he went over to the bank and got five new one hundred dollar bills and gave them to me, and I carried them around in my wallet for a long time, as long as I could, until I had to use them for eating money.

The Wright brothers' act of concentration was in harnessing of the air with a heavier than air airplane. Sears Roebuck and Company's concentration was upon developing a reliable mail-order merchandising business. Back in the days when it first started, if you sent your money away by mail for merchandise, the chances are you would never hear about it, and if you did get the merchandise, oftentimes it was not as good as recommended, and you couldn't do anything about it. That great house of Sears Roebuck and Company established confidence on the part of the public and built one of the greatest merchandising businesses known to mankind.

The concentration of the signers of the Declaration of Independence was to give personal liberties to all of the people of the world, and particularly of America. And every man who has failed, he is concentrating, or should be, upon how to succeed. There is where this philosophy comes to his rescue. We have created a philosophy that enables the man who has been a failure in the past to become a success in the future. And every living creature below the intelligence of man concentrates upon how to protect his life and how to get something to eat.

Those are some of the things that are actively associated with controlled attention.

Controlled attention is the act of focusing the mind on a given desire until ways and means for its realization have been worked out and successfully put into operation. Success comes after much concentration. Controlled attention to the power of our thoughts and to the energy we can generate through the mind is a vital tool.

Prayer is not only worship. It is a form of controlled attention. Prayer generates power, energy, unity, and strength. Thinking with another on a certain subject brings new insights, new truths. Attention focused by one individual or several brings power.

The principles one must apply in order to get the greatest benefits from the principle of controlled attention are:

1. Definiteness of purpose
2. The master mind
3. Applied faith
4. The habit of going the extra mile
5. Personal initiative
6. Self-discipline
7. Creative vision
8. Accurate thinking
9. Learning from defeat
10. Enthusiasm
11. Pleasing personality

I will now give you the principles which, when combined in the mind, through controlled attention, produce mind power bordering upon the miraculous:

1. Definiteness of purpose
2. Self-discipline through control of the emotions
3. Autosuggestion applied to the attainment of one's purpose
4. The power of the will, actively engaged and directed to a definite end

5. Personal initiative

6. Creative vision

7. Applied faith

The power of controlled attention or concentration is a product of the will and is related to self-discipline. Concentration saves one from the dissipation of his energies and aids him in keeping his mind focused upon the object of his definite major purpose until it has been taken over by the subconscious section of the mind and there made ready for translation to its physical equivalent through the law of cosmic habit force. It is the camera's eye of the imagination through which the detailed outline of one's aim and purposes are recorded in the subconscious section of the mind. Hence, it is indispensable.

Narrator: *Enthusiasm, our second principle for discussion today, is often confused with animated feeling. You cannot get enthusiasm from jumping up and down on a table or running around the house. As Dr. Hill has explained, real enthusiasm comes from within and is faith in action. Dr. Hill, what are some of the benefits of enthusiasm?*

Dr. Hill: I think I can best answer that question by telling you how to develop enthusiasm—first of all, by action based upon a burning desire. What is a burning desire? A desire so determined, so definite that you're willing to pay any price for the attainment of the object of it. It is quite distinct and separate from mere hopes and wishes. A burning desire is the beginning of enthusiasm. There is active enthusiasm and passive enthusiasm. Active enthusiasm is more effective than passive.

Public speakers and teachers can express enthusiasm by the control of their voice. One must feel enthusiasm before being able to express it. It's something that's got to come from within. One should practice the development of enthusiasm in daily conversations. A speech in monotones is always boring. Facial expression should also express enthusiasm through the properly directed smile. Start now, if you please, to observe people who express enthusiasm in their conversational relations and people who do not. You'll get a great lesson in attractiveness of personality.

Form definite habits by which you will learn to express enthusiasm in your ordinary conversations. Practice before a mirror. Practice by talking to yourself. When you express enthusiasm in your daily conversations, observe with profit how others pick up your enthusiasm and reflect it back to you as their own. Enthusiasm, in other words, is a contagious thing. If you give it out, it comes back to you. It comes back to you greatly multiplied.

When you meet with any sort of unpleasant circumstance, learn to transmute that circumstance into a pleasant feeling by repeating your definite major purpose in life with great enthusiasm and repeating that definite major purpose over and over again. Repetition has a very great power.

Narrator: *Dr. Hill can quote from memory many of Ralph Waldo Emerson's writings. It was Emerson who said, "Every great and commanding moment in the annals of the world is a triumph of some enthusiasm." Doctor, you've seen this demonstrated a good many times in your lifetime, haven't you?*

Dr. Hill: I not only have seen it demonstrated, but I have also demonstrated it myself. For instance, back in the early days when I wanted to get a job from a certain firm while I was going to high school, here's the way I went about it: I wrote an application stating my qualifications and my desire for the job. The answer came back "No. Sorry, no position open." Next I sent a telegram. The answer was still "No." Next, I sent a special delivery letter every day for a week. The answer was still "No." Next, I sent a special delivery telegram every hour for two days, and the firm telegraphed me to come and go to work.

Then there was Clarence Saunders, one of my outstanding students of Memphis, Tennessee. Clarence delivered groceries, and he had a great amount of enthusiasm and also a keen imagination. He was constantly trying to interest his employer in new and improved methods of merchandising, and finally the employer became so peeved at Clarence for wasting his time with what he called "foolish suggestions" that he told him that if he came in with another one, he was going to fire him. Shortly thereafter, the first cafeteria in the city opened in Memphis, Tennessee. When Clarence went out to his lunch that day, he saw a great line of people extending out onto the sidewalk waiting to be served in the cafeteria. Out of curiosity, he got on the end of the line, and when he picked up his tray and filled it up, by the time he got down to the cashier, his imagination began to churn. He said, "What a wonderful thing this would be in our grocery business, to have a self-help grocery store so women could come in with a basket on their arm, pick up what they wanted, and pay for it at one place as they went out. It would save a lot of time and it would save a lot of embarrassment." Clarence could hardly wait until he got back to the store, and he rushed in and said, "Well, boss, I have a multimillion dollar idea."

The boss said, "Clarence, you are fired."

Clarence said, "Oh no, I'm not. I resigned before I started to talk." Later on, I talked with the man who was Clarence's boss, and he said as near as he could figure, every word that he used in trying to fire Clarence had cost him a million dollars, because Clarence took his idea of self-help grocery stores to a firm which financed it under the name of Piggly Wiggly stores, and he made four million dollars during the first four years—an astounding illustration of what a man can do with an idea backed by the proper amount of enthusiasm.

Enthusiasm is a state of mind that inspires and arouses one to put action into the task at hand. It does more than this. It is contagious and vitally effects not only the enthusiast but all with whom he comes in contact. Enthusiasm is the vital moving force that impels action. The greatest leaders of men are those who know how to inspire enthusiasm in their followers. Enthusiasm is the most important factor entering into salesmanship. It is by far the most vital factor that enters into public speaking. The finest lecture ever delivered would fall upon deaf ears if it were not backed with enthusiasm by the speaker.

Enthusiasm is the vital force with which you recharge your body and develop a dynamic personality. Some people are blessed with natural enthusiasm, while others must acquire it. The way to develop it is simple. It begins by the doing of the work or rendering of the service which one likes best. Happiness, the object of all human effort, is a state of mind that can be maintained only through the hope of future achievement. Happiness lies always in the future and never in the past. The happy person is the one who dreams of heights of achievement that are yet unattained. The home you intend to own, the money you intend to earn and place in the bank, the trip you intend to take when you can afford it, the position in life you intend to fill when you have prepared yourself, and the preparation itself—these are the things that produce happiness. Likewise, these are the materials out of which your definite major purpose is formed. These are the things over which you may become enthusiastic no matter what your present station in life may be.

Enthusiasm is a contagious state of mind which not only aids one in gaining the cooperation of others but, more important than this, inspires the individual to draw upon and use the power of his own imagination. It inspires action also in the expression of personal initiative and leads to the habit of concentration of endeavor. Moreover, it is one of the qualities of major importance of a pleasing personality. In addition to all of these benefits, enthusiasm gives force and conviction to the spoken word. Enthusiasm is the product of motive, but it is difficult to maintain without the aid of the other principles.

There is a difference between inspired feeling and animated feeling. Animated feeling can be quickly acquired at a pep rally or sales meeting by external influence on the individual. You can easily acquire this feeling by singing, running around the house, jumping up and down and shouting or through self-control. Likewise, animated feeling can be quickly lost. You can turn it on or shut it off like an electric light. Enthusiasm or inspired feeling is hard to stop. It cannot be turned on or off at will. This faith in action will move the salesman over virtually any obstacle that he might encounter. With it he can literally accomplish the impossible.

Enthusiasm puts into practice the premise "Whatever the mind of man can conceive and believe, it can achieve." Enthusiasm causes one to glow. This radiant feeling is contagious. It will be grasped at once by your prospect and others that come into contact with you, and they will reflect it right back to you as their own feeling. Every successful salesman must have enthusiasm. Indeed, every successful person must have enthusiasm. Enthusiasm is the utilization of the spirit within you and the ability to tap this great inner source of intelligence. Enthusiasm is no more, no less than faith in action.

I will now list the ten benefits of controlled enthusiasm:

1. It sets up the vibrations of thought and thereby makes the faculty of the imagination more alert

2. It clears the mind of negative emotions by transmuting them into positive emotions, thereby preparing the way for the expression of faith

3. It aids the digestive organs in functioning normally

4. It gives a pleasing, convincing color to the tone of the voice

5. It definitely takes the drudgery out of labor

6. It adds to the attractiveness of the personality

7. It inspires self-confidence

8. It aids in the maintenance of sound physical health

9. It becomes of major importance in transmuting negative emotion into positive emotion

10. It gives the necessary force to one's desires and thereby influences the subconscious section of the mind to act with promptness on these desires.

If you wish to develop controlled enthusiasm, take these nine steps:

1. First, adopt a definite major purpose and a definite plan for attaining it and go to work carrying out the plan now.

2. Back the purpose with an obsessional desire, an enthusiastic motive for its attainment. Let the desire become a burning desire.

3. Write out a clear statement of your definite major purpose and the plan by which you hope to attain it, together with a statement of what you intend to give in return for its realization.

4. Follow the plan through with persistence based on all the enthusiasm you can generate.

5. Keep as far away as possible from joy killers and confirmed pessimists. Substitute in their place associates who are optimistic, and do not mention your plans to anyone except those in full sympathy with you.

6. If the nature of your definite major purpose requires it, and it almost always does, ally yourself with others whose aid you require.

7. If you're overtaken by temporary defeat, study your plans carefully, and if need be, change them, but do not change your major purpose.

8. Never let a day pass without taking some time to carry out your plans. The habit of enthusiasm calls for repetition through physical action.

9. Autosuggestion is a powerful factor in the development of any habit; therefore, keep yourself sold on the belief that you will obtain the object of your definite major purpose. Keep your mind positive at all times, remembering that enthusiasm thrives only on a positive mind.

Enthusiasm is an emotion, the physical counterpart to our ideas. It begins and ends in our minds. Enthusiasm is harmony. Enthusiasm is confidence. When you feel yourself taking hold of a definite idea, a definite plan, then you become enthusiastic. Enthusiasm is a feeling of confidence, an awareness of a relationship between oneself and the source of power to achieve. Speak with enthusiasm and positiveness. Move with confidence and observe how enthusiasm grows and spreads to others.

From this day forward, your duty to yourself requires that you do something each day to improve your technique for the expression of enthusiasm. Practice, practice, and practice until you will attain perfection. And just remember that an ounce of enthusiasm is worth a million pounds of mere knowledge when it comes to selling yourself through life. No man ever becomes a master salesman until he learns to express enthusiasm at will. "Enthusiasm," said Emerson, "is a requirement of all great achievements."

Chapter 7

Imagination, Adversity and Defeat, Budgeting Time and Money

Narrator: *The imagination is the workshop of the soul wherein is shaped all plans for individual achievement. I know that you recognize that gem, Dr. Hill; you wrote it. Would you comment further on its significance?*

Dr. Hill: Yes, I did write it, and I've seen it put into action many times. Suppose that you are an employee working for a firm. Here are some questions which might put your imagination to work very beneficially. First of all, create a plan which will help any employee do a better job. If you can do that, you can up your salary almost instantly.

- Can you show the company how it can save money on any operation without impairing the same?

- Can you suggest to the company some item of merchandise it could manufacture and market at a profit?

- Can you suggest a plan which would serve to give the public in and near the city in which you live a better appreciation of what the company means to the community financially?

- Can you suggest an idea which would make you happier in your job and worth more to the company?

- Can you suggest five rules of conduct which would make anyone more popular with his or her associates?

- Can you name five benefits you might receive by following the habit of going the extra mile—that is, rendering more service and better service than you're paid to render, and doing it in a positive pleasing mental attitude?

- Can you give a practical definition of your idea of success? What would be that definition? My definition would be that success is the ability to get from life whatever you want without violating the rights of other people.

- Can you name the most important cause of success?

- Can you name five things you could do which might bring you a promotion and more pay?

- Can you say definitely, first, what position you wish to be holding five years from now; second, what income you hope to be earning; and third, what sort of home you expect to be living in?

- Can you name three things which make our American way of life superior to the ways of all other people?

- Whom do you believe to be the most important person living? That answer should interest you very greatly because the truth is that as far as you are concerned, you are the most important person now living.

- What are your rules for making and keeping friends?

- Who does the promoting—the employee or the employer?

- What are your rules for earning promotions?

- Can an employee get more by griping and faultfinding than he can by friendly cooperation with the management?

- Do you dislike people who do not agree with you and your ideas in general?

- Do you know what is your greatest fault and your greatest virtue?

- What would you say is the most important asset that you control?

- Can you control your mental attitude at will? If so, how would you do it?

- Do you think for yourself or allow others to sway you into their way of thinking?

- Can you name the ten people who have made the greatest contributions to what we call the American way of life?

- Who, in your opinion, is our present day greatest business and industrial leader and why? If you can answer all of these questions correctly, you will have developed a marvelous capacity for using your imagination.

Narrator: *Dr. Hill, why don't more people today let their glorious minds soar into the realm of creativity?*

Dr. Hill: As a matter of fact, the main purpose of the Science of Personal Achievement is to enable more people to do just that. The reason more people are not using their imagination is that they haven't had the privilege, perhaps, of mastering and applying the Science of Personal Achievement.

Imagination is the workshop of the human mind, wherein old ideas and established facts may be reassembled into new combinations and put to new uses. It is the act of constructive intellect in grouping the materials of knowledge or thought into new, original, and rational systems; the constructive or creative faculty embracing poetic, artistic, philosophic, scientific, and ethical imagination. Creative vision may be an inborn quality of the mind or it may be an acquired quality, for it may be developed by the free and fearless use of the faculty of imagination. It has been said, "Imagination is the workshop of the soul wherein is shaped all plans for individual achievement."

Creative vision expressed by men and women who have been unafraid of criticism has been responsible for the civilization of today as we know it. From the days of the signing of the Declaration of Independence to the present, the American way of life has evolved through the efforts of men who were inspired to action through creative vision. Men of vision—we call them philosophers—foretell the future by looking backward into the past. Isn't it wonderful that our nation is a land of opulence and opportunity because it is operated under a system of government and a system of free enterprise which have encouraged men who have creative vision?

There are two types of imagination; let's look at them. First, synthetic imagination, consisting of a combination of the recognized ideas, concepts, plans, or facts arranged in a new order or put to a new use. Basically, new ideas are rarely revealed, and they are never revealed except to those with creative vision. Nearly every fact or idea known to or used by modern civilization is but a combination of something old which has been rearranged in a new combination. Secondly, we have creative imagination which has its base in the subconscious section of the mind, as the medium by which entirely new ideas are generated.

One of the ways to increase your flow of ideas is developing the habit of the silent hour when you will be still and listen for that small voice that speaks from within, thus discovering the greatest of all powers, creative vision—the one power that can shift one from the failure side of the river of life over to the success side.

Man's greatest gift is his thinking mind. It analyzes, compares, chooses. It creates, visualizes, foresees, and generates ideas. Imagination is your mind's exercise, its challenge, its adventure.

Narrator: *A statement that many persons find difficult to accept until they become students of this success philosophy is "Every adversity carries with it the seed of an equivalent or a greater benefit." Dr. Hill, would you explain this great truism?*

Dr. Hill: Yes, it's true that failure, fear, physical pain, and all other forms of adversity carry with them the seed of an equivalent or greater benefit. Physical pain is the common language of nature, in which she speaks to all living creatures and teaches them many things they would not learn in any other way. Failure and defeat have been known to turn people back from chosen pursuits which, had they been attained, would have led to destruction.

Remember the next time you meet with any sort of adversity that it contains the seed of an equivalent or greater benefit, but you must find that seed and germinate it into growth in your behalf through constructive thinking and positive action. Every circumstance affecting your life can be turned to a benefit by your mental attitude toward it.

Now let me give you some illustrations. Take the case of the defeat of Lord Cornwallis by the armies of George Washington in 1778. Probably it was considered by the British to have been an irreparable loss from which no benefits would ever come, but the defeat turned out to have been a blessing in disguise, because the United States of America, born of that defeat, saved the British empire from possible total destruction in both World Wars I and II, not to mention having also helped to feed the British people when they were hungry and sorely in need of the aid which they so recently received in overabundance.

Take the case of Abraham Lincoln. In his early life, Lincoln fell in love with Ann Rutledge, probably the only woman whom he ever loved, and when Ann Rutledge died, Lincoln's sorrow became so great that his friends thought he would lose his mind. He was missing for a couple of days, and he was finally located spread out across the grave of Ann Rutledge, weeping. One of the facts overlooked by those who wrote about Lincoln's life is that had it not been for the sorrow which Lincoln felt over the death of his sweetheart, he would not have become the great man that he was. That sorrow reached deeply into the depths of his soul and revealed a man who later became one of the greatest presidents of the United States.

And take Charles Dickens. His sorrow over the loss of his first sweetheart led him to transmute this sorrow into writing, and his first book, *David Copperfield*, and many other books, became classics for all time to come. And take O Henry—his real name was William Porter—who found himself in prison in Columbus, Ohio, and as a result of that adversity, turned his attention to writing and turned out books which immortalized him.

And take my son, Blair, who was born without any sign of ears. He was trained to believe that it was not an adversity, that it was a blessing, because it would cause people to recognize his condition and they'd go out of their way to be kind to him, and that's exactly the way it turned out. I have often said that the adversity that befell my son, Blair, made it possible for him to get through life with less resistance than his brothers, who have all of their faculties.

Adversity. I can tell you had it not been for the many adversities which I experienced in the early part of my work with Andrew Carnegie, I never would have completed the Science of Personal Achievement. I had adversity after adversity, but I learned to transmute those adversities into something constructive, to come up with something that would take the place of the adversity. Every time I failed, I said, "Well, this is just another opportunity that I have to prove that my philosophy can take care of the situation of failure." I learned to transmute all failures into successes. I also learned the difference between temporary defeat and failure. Most people accept defeat as permanent failure. Defeat is never failure. No circumstance is ever failure until it is accepted by the individual as such. That's one of the greatest things that I learned about this principle of profiting by adversity.

Adversity is a part of life. Every act, situation, or choice of our lives contains cause and effect. In adversities, we have situations in which we are made very much aware of the effect. The cause may be known, or it may be elusive or incomprehensible. We experience a very personal significant reaction, a strong emotion is stirred within us, and we ask, "Why?" Every adversity carries within it the seed of an equivalent or greater benefit. If we can capture this truth and can accept the fact that this universe is governed by immutable laws which are part of the creative force, no matter how difficult it may be to see the reason, then we can ride out any storm which besets our lives. Your attitude in time of adversity determines much of its effect on your life for good or ill. Defeat may be a steppingstone or a stumbling block according to the mental attitude in which one relates himself to it. The great man of letters, Emerson, said, "Our strength grows out of our weakness."

There are two types of defeat. One is the sort of defeat which one experiences in connection with material things—the loss of money, the loss of a position, the loss of property, or opposition growing out of friction in human relationships. The other is defeat from within where one loses contact with the spiritual forces of his being, is overcome by discouragement, fear, worry, or anxiety, and gives up and quits trying. The river of life is likened to the wheel on which the affairs of men revolve: a great river, one half of which flows in one direction and carries all who enter it to inevitable success, while the other half flows in the opposite direction and as definitely carries all who enter it to failure and defeat.

The river is not imaginary but real. It exists in the power of human thought and dwells in the mind of man, which is the one and only thing over which human beings have been provided with full and complete right of unchallenged and unchallenge-able control. The success side is attainable through definiteness of purpose, applied faith, the master mind, and a willingness to go the extra mile—the big four of the seventeen principles of individual achievement. Attainment of this great cooperative power may be aided by the remaining principles of this philosophy, but the big four are of major importance. Recognize this truth, and you will understand why many men go all the way through life in the failure side of the stream, while others who seem to have less or no greater ability are swept on to success with apparent ease.

The major burden of all the principles of this philosophy is that of providing the means by which one may cross over from the failure side of the stream to the success side. For it is inevitable that every person must find himself on the negative side of the stream at one time or another, sometimes because of circumstances over which he has no immediate control. All of these and many more circumstances that are unavoidable may, and often do, overtake men—circumstances which are clearly beyond one's immediate control. Yet each and every one of them carries with it the seed of equivalent benefit.

Success without humility of the heart is apt to prove only temporary and unsatisfying. Evidence of this may be found in most instances where people become suddenly successful without the experience of hardship, struggle, and temporary defeat—the great disciplinarian forces of mankind. All people who have been accepted by the world as successes have undergone defeat comparable with the scope of their success. Such men have learned to use the winds of adversity to sail their ships of life. You can too if you believe you can.

The good Lord made us to grow strong through struggle, and it would be a great pity if nobody had any problems at all. You would never grow if you didn't have problems. If you want a strong arm, do you tie it up to your side and take it out of use and let it rest?

Is that the way you develop a strong arm? Or do you hang a ten pound hammer on it and give it systematic use? And out of that resistance comes strength. It's the same thing with this part of your anatomy up here. Struggle is one of the greatest things on earth. I think I have failed in my early days more than all the rest of you here combined—much more—and had it not been for those failures and what I learned from them in the way of coming back, making a comeback, I wouldn't be standing here talking to you.

Don't mind problems. The good Lord gave you problems for a reason, problems that you had to exert yourself to overcome through effort and through struggle. I'm not talking about the Napoleon Hill philosophy now; I'm talking to you about the philosophy of the good Lord. That's the way He operates; He gives us problems.

Narrator: *We have reached the twelfth gate in our Science of Personal Achievement. After we pass through this gate, we shall know how to make the most of our time and how to acquire money and make it serve a noble purpose. I have always been impressed, Dr. Hill, with this statement that you've made many times: "Tell me how you use your spare time and I'll tell you where and what you will be ten years from now." Will you tell us how you can accomplish these forecasts?*

Dr. Hill: First of all, let us analyze the twenty-four hours a day which each of us have at our disposal. We have eight hours for sleep, and you can't do anything about that because nature demands that price for your health and your welfare. Then we have eight hours for work, as a rule. We need that for making a living and for accumulating money for old age protection and so forth. Then we have eight hours for recreation and spare time activities.

These hours are our own; we can do with them as we please. The sixteen hours allotted to work and sleep are on the "must" list and are partially or wholly out of the control of the individual. The eight hours of spare time belong to the individual for whatever use that is desired. In these eight hours will be found the cause of both success and failure, depending upon the use made of them.

Here are some suggestions for budgeting income and expenses. It makes no difference how much a man earns—if he doesn't set aside a definite percentage off of the top of the income for savings, he'll wind up with no money sooner or later. The monthly or weekly amount of income should be distributed as follows:

1. A definite percentage, generally not less than 10 percent of gross income, should be invested in life insurance. This is particularly true of a man who has a young and growing family, who has children to be educated later on in life.

2. A definite percentage for food, clothing, and housing. This should be in proportion to a man's income or his capacity to earn.

3. A definite amount to be set aside for investment because the more successful people in the world have learned how to make their money work for them while they sleep and while they're awake as well.

Whatever amount remains after these three "musts" have been allotted should go into a current checking or spending account for emergencies, recreation, education, and so forth. Ponder well the suggestions I am making because if you don't control your life by a budgeting system, you may be sure that you'll wind up without anything to protect you in old age.

Since your day has the same twenty-four hours in it as everyone else's in the world, you have the same opportunity as anyone for the skilled use of this time. Man has always had to harmonize with the world around him. In every generation, man has had to cope with the changing tides and tempos of the world around him, but as the demands are made, the balance is there if we seek it out. There is less time now because automation and faster transportation and communication seem to rush us. The art of budgeting time is one of the hardest to master but most rewarding.

There's a difference between the drifter and the non-drifter. The non-drifter has a plan, a definite major purpose, and a definite plan for its attainment and is busily engaged in carrying out that plan. He thinks his own thoughts and assumes full responsibility for them, right or wrong. He is a leader in his chosen occupation. He takes pride in blazing new trails, mastering new hazards, and learning from his mistakes and failures. The drifter does no real thinking but accepts the thoughts, ideas, and opinions of others and acts on them as if they were his own. He is at the mercy of a non-drifter in all ways of life and under all circumstances. He is a follower. He follows the line of least resistance on all occasions and repeats his mistakes over and over again. The drifter usually is as careless with his money as he is with his time. He fails to recognize that time is the same as money, and he spends both with a reckless disregard for their value.

Andrew Carnegie said, "The value of all riches, money included, consists in the use one makes of them, not in their possession." Our spare time is so important that it is no exaggeration of the facts to say that the person who organizes and uses his spare time wisely thereby ensures himself against failure. Every man is looking for ways to find peace of mind in his golden years with money to take care of his needs. There is a definite way to provide against the inconveniences and the disgrace of poverty. It begins with recognition of the value and the proper usage of time. Oh what a headache one gets at the mention of saving of time and the conservation of money. Nearly everyone wishes to spend both time and money freely, but budget and conserve them? Never. However, independence and freedom of body and mind, the two great desires of all mankind, cannot become enduring realities without the self-discipline of a strict budgeting system. Hence this principle is, of necessity, an important essential of the philosophy of individual achievement.

Chapter 8

Positive Mental Attitude and Accurate Thinking

Narrator: *The number thirteen is considered by many to be unlucky. This can certainly be true if you fail to heed the advice given in our thirteenth principle, positive mental attitude. In this session, Dr. Hill gives the fifty steps necessary for the attainment of a positive mental attitude. I'd like to ask the world-famous author and philosopher to explain what he means by the two sealed envelopes that each of us bring with us at birth. Dr. Hill.*

Dr. Hill: At birth, we come over with the equivalent of two sealed envelopes. In one of these envelopes is a long list of the benefits and riches that one may receive by the positive use of his mind and in the other envelope, an equally long list of the penalties he must pay if he neglects to use his mind constructively. Nature abhors idleness and vacuums. Nature sees to it that strength grows out of struggle and effort, and she wants man to use his mind and to use it constructively. Nothing constructive and worthy of man's efforts ever has been or ever will be achieved except through that action which comes from a positive mental attitude based upon a definite purpose and activated by a burning desire and intensified until the burning desire is elevated to the plane of applied faith. Wishes, well, everyone has a flock of them. Idle curiosity, everyone has some of it. Hopes, perhaps half of the people have hopes for as yet unattained things or circumstances. A burning desire, only that small percentage of people who can be called successful ever feel the urge of this. Applied faith, only the leaders attain this degree of mind control, which can exist only with a positive mental attitude.

Prayer brings positive results only when it is expressed in a positive mental attitude. The most effective prayer is that which is expressed by individuals who have conditioned their minds to habitually think in terms of a positive mental attitude. The vibrations of thought sent out from an individual's mind carry with them to other minds the precise state of mind in which they are released, a fact well known to all master salesmen who have learned how to condition their minds and the minds of their prospective buyers even before seeing them.

No one can successfully teach the Science of Personal Achievement while in a negative mental attitude, and no student can profit by it while he's in a negative mental attitude. No lawyer can convince a jury, no clergyman can inspire his parishioners, no speaker can hold and influence his audience without the aid of a positive mental attitude, and it's been said that the most successful doctors in all branches of therapy are those who treat their patients with a positive mental attitude. The subconscious mind of an individual can be educated to produce constructive results only when it is given instructions in a positive mental attitude.

Everyone desires to be rich, but not everyone knows what constitutes enduring riches, and most people believe riches consist only of material things that money can buy. Here is a list of the twelve things which constitute real riches:

1. A positive mental attitude. Observe that it heads the list.

2. Sound physical health.

3. Harmony in human relations.

4. Freedom from fear.

5. The hope of future achievement.

6. The capacity for applied faith.

7. Willingness to share one's blessings with others.

8. Engagement in a labor of love.

9. An open mind on all subjects toward all people.

10. Complete self-discipline.

11. Wisdom with which to understand people.

12. Financial security. Observe, if you will, with great benefit the fact that money comes at the end of the list of the twelve things that make men rich.

A positive mental attitude is the starting point of all riches, whether they be riches of the material nature or intangible riches. It attracts the riches of true friendship and the riches one finds in the hope of future achievement. It provides the riches one may find in nature's handiwork as it exists in the moonlit night, in the stars that float in the heavens, in the beautiful landscapes, and in distant horizons; and the riches to be found in the labor of one's choice where expression may be given to the highest plane of man's soul; and the riches of harmony in home relationships where all members of the family work together in a spirit of friendly cooperation; and the riches of sound physical health which is the treasure of those who have learned to balance work with play, worship with love, and who have learned the wisdom of eating to live rather than of living to eat; and the riches of freedom from fear; and the riches of enthusiasm, both active and passive; and the riches of song and laughter, both of which indicate states of mind; and the riches of self-discipline, through which one may have the joy of knowing that the mind can and will serve any desired end if one will take possession and command it through definiteness of purpose.

Our mind is the only thing we can control. Either we control it, or we relinquish control and we drift. We can do something about any situation. We cannot not do anything. Being negative is doing something. To govern your life, you must learn to govern your attitude. How we react is determined by our habits of mind control and our attitudes. Are you looking for positive avenues to success? Then a positive mental attitude will divert you to the positive side of the street.

Now let's look at the nine important benefits resulting from developing a positive mental attitude. The first is taking control of one's mind. Secondly, a positive mental attitude permits us to get on the success beam. Third, a positive mental attitude develops a success consciousness. Fourth, a positive mental attitude gives complete protection against fear and worry. Fifth, a positive mental attitude promotes expression of applied faith and makes available forces of infinite intelligence, the foundation on which all prayer should be expressed. Sixth, with a positive mental attitude, we can meet our other self, which knows no self limitations. Seventh, a positive mental attitude makes possible an expression of the creative emotion of love. Eighth, a positive mental attitude permits us to write our own ticket in life and be sure it will pay off on our own terms. And ninth, a positive mental attitude is the only condition of the mind in which we can have wisdom with which to recognize the true purpose of life and adapt ourselves to that purpose.

Here are the fifty steps necessary to condition your mind so it will express a positive mental attitude automatically at all times:

1. Recognize the privilege of taking possession of your own mind.

2. Recognize that every adversity, failure, or defeat, of your own making or otherwise, carries the seed of equal or greater benefit and may be transmuted into blessings of great proportions.

3. Close the door behind you on all failures and unpleasant circumstances and make room for a positive mental attitude.

4. Begin now helping others acquire benefits similar to your desires by going the extra mile.

5. Select a pacemaker.

6. Determine material riches you require. Don't develop greed.

7. Form the habit of saying or doing something to make others feel better every day.

8. Don't take yourself too seriously.

9. Perform a labor of love, preferably in your daily work or a hobby.

10. To solve your problem, help others solve theirs, and a solution to yours will be revealed.

11. Read Emerson's essay on compensation until understood and assimilated to condition your mind for a positive mental attitude.

12. Make a list of all your assets, not only material ones, noting especially a sound mind to shape your destiny.

13. Immediately and always seek forgiveness from those you have offended.

14. Recognize that your space in this world will depend on the quality of service you render and the mental attitude in which you render it.

15. By breaking objectionable habits, you become the boss of your life.

16. Remember, no one can hurt your feelings or anger or frighten you without your full consent. Don't let them. Close your mind to these irritations. Act, don't react.

17. Become master of the love emotion by transmutation.

18. Depend on yourself. Eliminate self-pity.

19. Study this lesson once a week for six months to condition your mind to remain positive.

20. Always be yourself.

21. Be selective in clothes to express your personality.

22. Read all of Emerson's essays.

23. Do not let death frighten you; rather, be prepared for it.

24. Consider every circumstance of life as for the best.

25. Direct your urge for unwarranted power over others to better control of your own mind.

26. Use your own mind in shaping your destiny. Keep your mind so busy on the things you desire that there will be no time to think of things you do not want.

27. Attune your mind to attract to you the things and circumstances you desire by expressing in a daily prayer your feeling of gratitude.

28. Demand some dividend from life every day, but be sure to recognize the desirable things of life you already have, and use them.

29. Keep your mind positive by not accepting circumstances of which you do not approve.

30. Don't let anyone make up your mind for you.

31. Personal power does not consist in material things.

32. The best way to receive is by giving.

33. Repair weaknesses in your mental equipment if anyone can hurt your feelings or make you angry against your will.

34. Form the habit of tolerance. Like people just as they are. Love is free.

35. Keep a diary of good deeds done on behalf of others.

36. Offset every favor done for you by a greater favor. It will give you the capacity to get everything you are entitled to receive.

37. Don't fear old age. Nature replaces youth with wisdom. The greatest achievements often come after age fifty.

38. Adopt the motto "Deeds, not mere words."

39. Accept the proposition that all your problems have a solution.

40. Welcome friendly criticism; encourage it.

41. Form a group for round table discussions of these lessons.

42. Only that person is free who establishes a proper system for controlling and directing his own thoughts. You can create such a system which will serve your personal needs by applying the seventeen principles of the Science of Personal Achievement.

43. Take note of people with a negative mental attitude, and you'll be challenged to acquire the habit of a positive mental attitude.

44. Don't envy those who excel you; use them as pacemakers.

45. Instead of just wishing or hoping, create a burning desire to obtain your objective and develop a positive mental attitude in the process.

46. Refrain from negative conversation.

47. Acquire an enduring belief in the existence of infinite intelligence, necessary to help you take possession of your own mind and direct it to whatever ends you may choose.

48. Acquire an enduring belief in your own ability to become free and self-determining as your greatest gift from your Creator and demonstrate this belief in appropriate actions.

49. Believe in the American way of life.

50. Choose your associates wisely, and rely on those with whom you are associated.

This fifty point conditioning process has many facets and many methods of approach which leave no room for the alibi that the way to the establishment of a positive mental attitude is unknown.

Now, let's look at additional benefits of a positive mental attitude:

1. There is no energy for a negative mental attitude.

2. The habit of harmony within oneself. Close the door of the mind to all conflicting thoughts, past defeats, fears, and unpleasant thoughts.

3. Sound physical health. A health consciousness.

4. Mastery of worries. Nothing is worth the cost of worry.

5. The habit of looking for good in others.

6. Control of one's dominating thoughts by deliberately filling the mind with positive thoughts and refusing space to negative thoughts. You do this by using the power of will fixed on a definite purpose.

7. Control of the tongue. Every word spoken leaves its footprints on the mind and becomes a part of one's character.

8. The habit of smiling when speaking tends to soften the words and modify the meaning. Someone has said, "You are not fully dressed until you wear a smile."

9. The habit of controlling the emotions and complete discipline of your emotions is the result of a positive mental attitude.

10. Hero worship. Aspire to emulate people you admire, either now living or historical characters, and let them

personally influence your life, either by reading their biographies or associating with them.

11. The habit of going the extra mile is the best way to develop a positive mental attitude by rendering useful service beyond that which is expected and for which you expect no direct compensation.

Narrator: *Dr. Hill, another of your famous quotations is "That which you think today becomes that which you are tomorrow." Recognizing the importance of thinking accurately, would you tell us about this miracle of thought?*

Dr. Hill: Let us examine some of the tests to be made in separating facts from fiction. The first step in accurate thinking is to determine what is fact and what is fiction or what is hearsay evidence. Scrutinize with unusual care everything you read in newspapers or hear over the radio or television, and form the habit of never accepting any statement as fact merely because you read it or heard it over the radio or television or heard it expressed by some person. Statements bearing some proportion of fact often are intentionally or carelessly colored to give them the erroneous impression of total factualness.

Next, scrutinize carefully everything you read in books, regardless of who wrote them, and never accept the works of any writer without asking the following questions and satisfying yourself as to the answers. First, is the writer a recognized authority on the subject he has covered? Second, did the writer have an ulterior or a self-interest motive other than that of imparting accurate information in writing? Third, is the writer a paid propagandist whose profession is that of organizing public opinion? Fourth, has the writer a profit interest or other interest in the subject on which he writes? Fifth, is the writer a person of sound judgement and not a fanatic on the subject on which he writes? Sixth, are there reasonably accessible sources from which the writer's statements may be checked and verified? And if so, be sure to check them. Seventh, before accepting as fact statements by others, ascertain the motive which prompted the statements. Eighth, ascertain also the writer's reputation for truth and veracity. Ninth, scrutinize with unusual care all statements made by people who have strong motives or objectives they desire to attain through their statements, and be equally careful about accepting as facts the statements of overzealous people who have the habit of allowing their imagination to run wild. Such people are known as radicals or crackpots. Tenth, learn to be cautious and to use your own judgement no matter who is trying to influence you. If a statement does not harmonize with your own reasoning power, if it is out of harmony with your experience, hold it up for further examination. Falsehood has a clear way of bringing with it some form of warning note, perhaps in the tone of one's voice or in the expression of one's face. This, when it is recognized, is known as intuition. Eleventh, in seeking facts from others, do not disclose to them what facts you expect to find because many people have the bad habit of trying to please, even if they have to fabricate in order to do it. Twelfth, science is the art of organizing and classifying facts. When you wish to make sure you're dealing with facts, seek scientific sources for their testing wherever possible. Men of science have neither the reason nor the inclination to modify or change facts or to misrepresent. Each of the seventeen principles of the Science of Personal Achievement were checked carefully by scientists to make sure of the soundness of the Science of Personal Achievement.

All thought, whether it is positive or negative, good or bad, accurate or inaccurate, tends to clothe itself in its physical equivalent, and it does so by inspiring one with ideas, plans, and the means of attaining desired ends through logical and natural means. Accurate thought involves two fundamentals, which all who indulge in it must observe. First, to think accurately, you must separate facts from mere information. There is much information available to you that is not based upon facts. Second, you must separate facts into two classes, namely the important and the unimportant or the relevant and the irrelevant. Only by so doing can you think clearly. All facts which you can use in the attainment of your definite major purpose are important and relevant. All that you cannot use are unimportant and irrelevant. It is mainly the neglect of some to make this distinction, which accounts for the chasm which separates so widely the accuracy of thought of people who appear to have equal ability and who have had equal opportunity.

Without going outside of your own circle of acquaintances, you can point to one or more persons who have had no greater opportunity than you have had and who appear to have no more or perhaps less ability than you who are achieving far greater success, and you wonder why. Search diligently, and you will discover that all such people have acquired the habit of combining and using the important facts which affect their line of work. Far from working harder than you, they are perhaps working less and with greater ease. By virtue of their having learned the secret of separating the important facts from the unimportant, they have provided themselves with a sort of fulcrum and lever which they can move with their little fingers. The power for all achievement, the power that you need in order to understand and apply the philosophy of success, is readily available. The power you need for a productive life is in the storehouse of your own mind.

The power of thought may be likened to a rich garden spot. The soil may be converted by organized effort into necessary products of food or, by neglect, it may be allowed to produce useless weeds. The mind is eternally at work, building up or tearing down, bringing misery, unhappiness, and poverty or joy, pleasure, and riches. It is never idle. It is the greatest of all the assets available to mankind, yet it is the least used and the most abused of all assets. Its abuse consists mainly in its nonuse.

Science has revealed many of nature's most profound secrets, but not the secret of man's great source of riches, the power of his own thoughts. This is one secret which has never been revealed to mankind, perhaps because mankind has shown such unpardonable indifference toward this divine gift. The power of thought is the most dangerous or the most beneficial power available to man, depending, of course, on how it is used. Through the power of thought, man builds great empires of civilizations. Through that same power, other men trample down empires as if they were so much helpless clay.

Every creation of man, whether it be good or bad, is created first in a thought pattern. All ideas are conceived through thought. All plans, purposes, and desires are created in thought, and thought is the only thing over which man has been given the complete privilege of control. Thought is the master of all other forms of energy because it is a form of energy which is mixed with intelligence. Thought holds the solution to every human problem. When it is properly used, thought is the greatest known remedy for all physical ailments. The accurate thinker recognizes all of the facts of life, both the good and the bad, and assumes the responsibility of separating and organizing the two, choosing those which serve his needs and rejecting all the others. He is not impressed by hearsay evidence. He is not the slave but the master of his own emotions. These are some of the traits of an accurate thinker. Study them carefully if you would become one who thinks accurately.

These traits are simple and easily understood but not so easily cultivated, for cultivation requires more self-discipline than the majority of men are willing to exercise. But the reward for accurate thinking is worth the effort required to obtain that reward. It consists of many values. Among them are peace of mind, freedom of mind, freedom of body, wisdom and understanding of the laws of nature, the material necessities of life, and above all, harmony with the great scheme of the universe as it is established and maintained by the Creator. No one can deny that the accurate thinker has established a working relationship with his God. Accurate thinking is a priceless asset which cannot be purchased with money or borrowed from others. It must be self attained through the strictest habits of self-discipline as they have been defined by successful men and women in many walks of life.

It is the rarest sort of experience to find a person anywhere at any time who lives his own life, thinks his own thoughts, develops his own habits, and makes even the slightest attempt to be himself. Observe those whom you know best, study their habits carefully, and you'll realize that most of them are merely synthetic imitations of other people, without a thought they can truthfully call their own. Most people trail along accepting and acting upon the thoughts and habits of others, very much as sheep tag along after one another over established paths. Once in a great while, some individual with a tendency toward accurate thinking will pull away from the crowd, think his own thoughts, and dare to be himself. When you find such a person, take note. You are face-to-face with a thinker.

Choose what you want to achieve. Determine how you will set about achieving it. Move toward that goal with definite positive awareness and with faith. This is accurate thinking. The accuracy of your thinking is affected by the hopes, fears, desires and attitudes you allow to stimulate you. Organize your mind. Be aware of the power of your mind. Keep it controlled and accurate.

Chapter 9

Sound Physical Health and Cooperation

Narrator: *Good health, a sense of well-being, and a purpose for living make any day beautiful. Without good health, all the flavors of the good things of life are dulled. The key which will coordinate all the principles in this study, and the catalyst which sets every idea into motion, could be identified as sound physical health. In the current popular vernacular, if we are programmed to motivation springing from stated goals and buttressed by strong self-discipline, then achievement is assured. Programming occurs in the mind and is set in motion in the acts of the physical body. One purpose of this session is to alert your mind to the tremendous power which is generated through the attention paid to the importance of sound health consciousness.*

We cannot separate the body and the mind, for they are one. Anything that affects the health and vigor of the mind will affect the body. In turn, anything that affects the health of our body will affect the mind. This point is so essential to our understanding of health that we must view man as a whole. Man is not a being with a mind and body; he is a being who is both mind and body. Man is to be understood and approached as a whole. But we are also part of the environment in which we live. We are born into a world of trees and mountains and moonlit skies, peopled with all forms of living things, even a grain of wheat.

Perhaps we can gain wisdom and insight into the handling of this being of ours by examining the world about us and how it functions so that we may swim with the river of life and not exhaust our energies fighting against it. As we are one with the world about us, so are we one with ourselves. And as we are affected by the world we live in and, in turn, affect that world, so our body influences our mind and, in turn, our mind influences our body. The proper perspective would suggest that the highest function of all living things is present in man and in none of the Creator's other products. We are the only intelligent animal, and with this power, we have been able to modify our environment and to learn its laws. We have only to conceive the idea and believe the idea to achieve the idea.

Dr. Hill, would you tell us why you consider sound physical health to be one of the essentials of continued success?

Dr. Hill: Sound physical health is an essential for success because a properly functioning mind can exist only in a sound body. I want to tell you that it's due to the habits that we have formed. Let me give you some of the habits which lead to sound physical health. Sound health begins, for example, with a health consciousness which, in turn, may be acquired by these suggestions in connection with the mental attitude. First, there must be no griping in family or occupation or relationship. Second, no hatred. It attracts reprisals in kind. Next, no gossip or slander. They attract reprisals. No fear. It indicates friction in human relationships. No talk about disease. It leads to the development of hypochondria, that is to say, imaginary ailments. No envy. It indicates the lack of self-reliance. All of these negative thoughts and emotions hurt digestion, which is essential in delivering good health throughout the body.

In connection with our eating habits, prepare the mind to aid you in eating with peace of mind. No worries, arguments, or unpleasantness at mealtimes. No overeating. It overworks the heart and the lungs and the liver and the kidneys and the other organs of the body. Eat a balanced ration with fruits and vegetables and plenty of water. Don't eat rapidly; it prevents proper mastication. And don't eat candy bars, peanuts, and snacks between meals or drink too many soft drinks. Water is nature's natural remedy for thirst. Liquor in excess is taboo at all times. Take vitamin tablets if needed to supply food deficiencies, but take them on doctor's prescriptions only to make sure you get the sort the body needs.

In connection with relaxation, you need play to ensure sound health; therefore, balance all work with an equal amount of play. Sleep eight hours out of every day. Train yourself not to worry over things you cannot remedy. Don't look for trouble because it will find you in its own way sooner or later. There are two kind of things about which people worry. One, things in connection with which they can do something, and the other, things in connection with which they cannot do anything. Don't waste your time on the second kind.

Hope. A person without hope is lost. Sound health inspires hope, and hope inspires sound health. Develop hope by daily prayer, not for more blessings but with thanks for those you already have, such as freedom as an American citizen, the privilege of acting on your own initiative, an opportunity to secure economic freedom according to your talents, the freedom to worship in your own way, sound physical and mental health, the time that lies ahead of you, and the hope of a better world in which to live.

Regarding drugs and nostrums, avoid them altogether. Throw away your aspirin and your headache tablets. Headache is nature's way of warning you that something needs correction.

Remember, sound health doesn't come from bottles but from fresh air, wholesome food, and wholesome thinking and living habits. And watch your weight. Fat people may be good-natured, as they have been represented to be, but they generally die too young. Fasting. Learn to doctor yourself nature's way by fasting for a few days when you begin to feel off-color physically. Fast during your vacation or holidays when you are not working, but do it under the direction of your doctor.

And work. Work must be a blessing because the Creator provided that every living creature must engage in it in one way or another or perish. Work should be performed in the spirit of worship. Work should be based on the hope of achievement of some definite major purpose in life; thus it becomes voluntary—a pleasure to be sought, not a burden to be endured. Work with a spirit of gratitude for the blessings it serves both in sound physical health and economic security and for the benefits it may provide one's dependents, thus embellishing it with love.

Faith. Learn to communicate with infinite intelligence from within and adapt yourself to the laws of nature as they are written all around you.

Habits. All habits are made permanent and work automatically through the operation of the law of cosmic habit force, which forces every living thing to become a part of the environmental influences in which it exists. You may fix the pattern of your thought habits and your physical habits, but cosmic habit force takes these over and carries them out to their logical conclusion.

Sound health begins with a health consciousness produced by a mind which thinks in terms of health and not in terms of illness, plus temperance of habits in eating and properly balanced physical activities. Harmony with others begins with oneself for it is true, as Shakespeare said, "To thine own self be true, and it must follow, as the night the day, thou canst not then be false to any man."

No man who fears anything is a free man. Fear is a harbinger of evil, and wherever it appears, one may find a cause which must be eliminated before he can enjoy good health. The greatest of all forms of happiness comes as the result of hope of achievement of some yet unattained desire. Poor beyond description is the person who cannot look to the future with hope that he will become the person he would like to be or with the belief that he will obtain the objective he has failed to reach in the past.

Faith is the connecting link between the conscious mind of man and the great universal reservoir of infinite intelligence. It is the fertile soil of the garden of the human mind wherein may be produced all of the riches of life. It is the eternal elixir which gives creative power and action to the impulses of thought. Faith is the basis of all so called miracles and of many mysteries which cannot be explained by logic or science. Faith is the spiritual chemical which, when it is mixed with prayer, gives one direct and immediate connection with infinite intelligence. Faith is the power which transmutes the ordinary energies of thought into their spiritual equivalent, and it is the only power through which the cosmic force of infinite intelligence may be appropriated to the uses of man.

He who has not learned the blessed art of sharing has not learned the true path of happiness, for happiness comes only by sharing. Let it be forever remembered that life may be embellished and multiplied by the simple process of sharing with others. And let it also be remembered that the space one occupies in the hearts of his fellow men is determined precisely by the service he renders through some form of sharing his blessings. Sound physical health provides a suitable housing place for the operation of the mind; hence, it is an essential for enduring success, assuming that the word "success" shall embrace all of the requirements for happiness.

Here again, the word "habit" comes into prominence, for sound health begins with a health consciousness that can be developed only by the right habits of living sustained through self-discipline. Sound health provides the basis for enthusiasm, and enthusiasm encourages sound health. So the two are like the hen and the egg. No one can determine which came into existence first, but everyone knows that both are essential for the production of either. Health and enthusiasm are like that. Both are essential for human progress and happiness.

Your emotions must be under control before you can be sure of maintaining sound physical health. Without this control, you're like a man on a runaway horse who cannot grasp the reins.

Control over your emotions must include both the negative and the positive emotions.

Let's look at the seven positive emotions first:

1. Love
2. Sex
3. Hope
4. Faith
5. Enthusiasm
6. Loyalty
7. Desire

Now, the seven negative emotions:

1. Fear
2. Jealousy
3. Hatred
4. Revenge
5. Greed
6. Anger
7. Superstition

Emotions are your action producing forces. They can lift you to the highest plane of achievement in your chosen calling or lower you to the depths of failure, depending upon the extent of your control over them. If you believe that only your negative emotions need control, dismiss this idea immediately. Your positive emotions can also lead you into excesses that destroy the power of a positive mental attitude. The emotions of love and sex require careful guidance because they are the most powerful of all the emotions and are the ones which get out of control most often. Form the habit of keeping your mind occupied with what you desire and keeping it off that which you do not desire. Your thoughts tend to manufacture the circumstances that occupy your mind most often. Think about good health, plan to attain it, believe you will achieve it, and your thoughts will lead you in that direction.

A great German philosopher set forth the following principles for living a well-balanced, healthy life: "Health enough to make work a pleasure, wealth enough to support your needs, strength enough to battle difficulties and overcome them, patience enough to toil until some good has been accomplished, grace enough to confess your sins and forsake them, charity enough to see the good in your neighbors, love enough to move you to be useful and helpful to others, faith enough to make real the things of God, hope enough to remove all fears concerning the future." Everyone needs a blueprint by which to build his life. This creed may give you the basis of one you can form for yourself, which will help you to make life pay off on your own terms without violating the rights of others. A daily creed helps one to keep before him a clear picture of the person he desires to become. It helps to give him the power of faith to meet and overcome obstacles along the way.

Your thoughts affect your health. Thoughts can make you sick or thoughts can move you toward good health, good attitudes, sound sleep, and good eating habits. Develop a consciousness of good health and well-being. Good thinking generates harmony within our bodies and generates physical manifestations of order and system.

Narrator: *Dr. Hill, let's now concentrate on the next of the seventeen principles, cooperation. How can cooperation be used effectively in the home or business life?*

Dr. Hill: Let us analyze the two forms of cooperation. There's cooperation by force or coercion, and there's voluntary cooperation based upon motive or motivation. Cooperation differs from the master mind principle in that it is based upon coordination of effort without necessarily involving the principle of definiteness of purpose or the elements of harmony and a single goal. Cooperation based on the master mind principle is the medium by which great personal power may be attained, and no one has ever acquired such power without the aid of this principle, a fact which places it in the category of indispensable for a person who is aiming at the higher brackets of personal achievement in any calling.

Cooperation is indispensable in four major relationships: 1) In the home; 2) in one's job or profession; 3) in social relationships; and 4) in support of our form of government and free enterprise.

Let's consider some examples of cooperation not based on the master mind principle. One is soldiers working under Army regulations. They do a splendid job of creating power through coordination of effort, but they do not necessarily follow the master mind principle of working in perfect harmony. Employees working under rules of employment, government officials working under laws of the nation, professional men such as lawyers, doctors, and dentists working under rules of the ethics of their profession and citizens of a nation controlled by a dictator—now those would be illustrations of cooperation not necessarily based upon the master mind.

Observe the manner in which cooperative effort assumes greater power when the principle of cooperation is combined with the master mind principle involving harmony based on a definite motive. Some examples of potential power under this combination are these:

- Government officials when working in harmony with and supported by a majority of the people, as in the case of Franklin D. Roosevelt's first term in office, when an emergency of an economic depression supplied motive for harmony and the motive was a desire for economic recovery affecting all of the people

- Employers and their employees with a motive such as that which inspired harmony in the Arthur Nash clothing company of Cincinnati when the company faced bankruptcy

- Andrew Carnegie and his twenty master mind allies working in harmony with all of the employees to establish the steel age by bringing down the price of steel

- Henry Ford in connection with his employees when he established his famous five-dollar-a-day minimum wage plan, when the prevailing minimum wage at that time was about two dollars and a half per day

What motives inspire cooperation? First, opportunity to get increased compensation and promotion—that is one of the outstanding motives that inspires employees to cooperate in a friendly way with employers. Next, recognition for personal initiative, pleasing personality, and outstanding work. It has been said, and I think truly so, that many people work harder for recognition and for praise than they will for money. And a system of friendly competition between departments in a business and in departments between individuals. Patriotism should be the strongest possible motive for cooperation. Hope of future benefits in the form of some yet unattained goal which can best be attained by mutual cooperation is another.

Andrew Carnegie's method of inspiring cooperation was based on four principles: First, he established a monetary motive through promotions and bonuses. Second was his question system. He never reprimanded any employee offensively but instead allowed the employee who deserved it to reprimand himself or herself through carefully directed questions. Third, he always had one or more men in training for his job, and several of them acquired it. Fourth, he never made decisions for his employees, but instead encouraged them to make their own decisions and to be responsible for the results thereof.

The American system of free enterprise gets friendly cooperation by the profit motive and personal promotions based on the free exercise of each individual's personal initiative. No other system yet devised has ever inspired personal initiative on so high a scale, and it is due in the main to this fact that we can call this the freest and the richest nation of the world. The one outstanding quality that typifies an American citizen is his right to exercise his personal initiative through any form of cooperation he chooses.

Successful living depends on cooperation. Cooperation depends upon six important points:

1. Recognition and acceptance that each person on the team has a unique contribution to make.

2. Providing each individual with benefits that result from the association.

3. Each individual is stimulated by an adequate personal motive, preferably positive.

4. Cooperation must be organized. Each individual supplies some specialized talent which other members of the team do not possess.

5. The team requires a leader who assumes responsibility for coordinating the factors which affect the group goal.

6. The leader assumes responsibility for maintaining harmony within the group.

Power grows out of knowledge—power in yourself, your mind power, and power in the team. Your knowledge should be expressed in action. Cooperation, like love and friendship, is something one may get by giving. There will be other generations who will follow your generation, and their lot in life will depend largely on the kind of inheritance we of this generation leave to them.

An old man traveling a lonely highway
Came at the evening cold and gray
To a chasm deep and wide
The old man crossed in the twilight dim
But he turned when he reached the other side
And builded a bridge to span the tide
"Old man," cried a fellow pilgrim near
"You're wasting your strength with building here
Your journey will end with the ending day
And you never again will pass this way.
You have crossed the chasm deep and wide.

Why build you a bridge at eventide?"
And the builder raised his old gray head,
"Good friend, on the path I have come," he said
There followeth after me today
A youth whose feet must pass this way.
This stream which has been a naught to me
To that fair haired boy may a pitfall be.
He too must cross in the twilight dim.
Good friend, I am building this bridge for him."

Until we become inspired with this broader spirit of team-work, the spirit which recognizes the oneness of our people and the fellowship of all mankind, we shall not be in a position to benefit individually by the principle of cooperative effort. Greed and selfishness are no part of this spirit. No system can long endure unless it is founded squarely on the golden rule philosophy of live and let live. We do know that any system of human relationships which survives must be based on common decency, justice, and a keen sense of fairness, which will all inspire every person to give the world the best he has. And it must provide the means of inspiring men to work together in a spirit of teamwork. It is a companion of the principle of going the extra mile.

Human relationships which are founded on a strict adherence to these principles are bound to be harmonious to all of the participants. Give cooperation and you will receive cooperation. When the spirit of teamwork is willing, voluntary, and free, it leads to the attainment of a power which is very great and enduring. To get enduring cooperation from others, one must relate himself to them in such a way that they work together freely and willingly and entirely of their own accord. The most prominent quality of man is his inborn desire for personal freedom and the freedom of exercising his personal initiative in whatever manner he chooses. If you're a close observer, you will have noticed that the individuals who have attained the highest degree of cooperation in their relationships with others are those who have achieved the greatest success in their own chosen callings.

Everywhere and in everything, friendly teamwork is a fundamental principle of growth and power. There is a certain state of mind that tends to make men akin, establishes rapport between their minds, and provides the power of attraction that often gains the friendly teamwork of others. Enthusiasm is the state of mind to which I refer. Think with me now on these epigrams which will help you develop more friendly cooperation.

- No man is entitled to give orders unless he knows how to take orders and carry them out.
- Willing cooperation produces enduring power while forced cooperation ends in failure.
- Friendly cooperation will get a man more than unfriendly agitation in any market.
- No man can succeed and remain successful without the friendly cooperation of others.
- Most men will respond more freely to a request than they will to an order.
- A man who can't take orders graciously has no business giving them.
- Remember that no one can hurt your feelings without your cooperation and willingness.

Chapter 10

Cosmic Habit Force
and Conclusion

Dr. Hill: We're on the last of the seventeen principles, cosmic habit force, and the reason it comes last is that it was the last one to be discovered. I had sixteen principles going for a long time, but I knew there was a missing link. There was a missing link because I could make this philosophy work part of the time but not all of the time, and now I can make it work all of the time, and I do. I want each of you to get a copy of Emerson's essays and to familiarize yourself with, particularly, his essay on compensation. You won't understand it the first time, but don't feel badly about that; it took me ten years to understand it. I got a hold of it in 1913 when I was advertising manager of the LaSalle Extension University in Chicago, and I started reading it. And every time I read it, I said, "The time will come when I will rewrite this essay in English that anybody can understand."

Ralph Waldo Emerson had a great mind, a very deep mind. It was too deep for the majority of people. And he had a great capacity for taking a concrete idea and reducing it into the abstract so that nobody could possibly understand it at first contact. I want to give you that warning in advance. Over and over and over again I said, "I'm going to rewrite this essay," and I fully intended to do it. So that's fifty-one years ago when I started doing that. I eventually forgot about my commitment, but my subconscious mind didn't forget about it. In 1937, after *Think and Grow Rich* came out, I commenced to get letters, telegrams, and telephone calls from all over the country congratulating me on the book, on its value and its benefits. So I said, "Well, by golly, I'm going to get that book and read it. Maybe that fellow's got something." I got off to myself and I started reading *Think and Grow Rich*. I disassociated myself from it entirely and started reading it just as if I had never seen it. About halfway through, the seeds that I had planted in my subconscious mind about rewriting Emerson's essay popped out in the form of just what I wanted. It first came over in the form of hypnotic rhythm, the law through which nature hypnotizes everything into becoming a part of the environment in which it dwells or lives or exists. I took that to my consultant and longtime friend, Mr. Francis I. DuPont, and as we were going over it, he said, "You've got the wrong title. With hypnotic rhythm, you've got the negative side of it; let's find the positive side." And within the time that I've been talking to you about this, the positive side came over.

I said, "Well, of course, that's the negative side; let's find the positive." The positive is cosmic habit force, meaning the comptroller of all the natural laws of the universe, the one natural law into which all other natural laws resolve themselves, just like the threads in a rope. All are individual threads, but they resolve themselves into a relationship called a rope. You'll find as you get into a better understanding of this law of cosmic habit force that it is comptroller of the natural laws of the universe.

I had often wondered, before I came across the real meaning of this law of cosmic habit force—I'd often wondered how in the world the Lord above managed to dust off the stars, hang out the moon, bring the sun up in the morning, and take it to bed at night, and I said, "Well, he must be a mighty busy fellow to do all of that." But when I came into a better understanding of this, I found out that this whole universe is run according to a definite precise plan. It operates automatically. And then I commenced to get a better understanding of the law of cosmic habit force.

You should understand that the other sixteen principles are a part and parcel of this law of cosmic habit force, and they depend upon it for their effective operation. When you have a better understanding of the law of cosmic habit force, you know why it's necessary for you not only to have a definite major object in life and minor objectives, but you'll also understand why I insist upon your writing out that definite major purpose just as laid down in Lesson Number One, commit it to memory, and repeat it over and over again from time to time until the subconscious mind picks up the pattern of what it is that you're after.

I mentioned my invisible guides in an earlier talk, and I fancy that the first time a person hears of that they think maybe I'm just a little bit screwy, especially if they don't understand the principle of autosuggestion. But once you come to understand this principle of autosuggestion and the law of cosmic habit force, you understand what I am doing when I create these imaginary entities to keep my mind focused on the things that I want to do in life.

The purpose of this entire course has been to enable one to establish habits that lead to financial security, health, and peace of mind necessary for happiness. In this lecture, we examine briefly the established law of nature which makes all habits permanent. With the application of the principles of this philosophy, one may set up a pattern of any desired habit, after which the habit is taken over by cosmic habit force and made to carry on automatically. Is that an astounding thing to recognize, that there is a law to which you can adjust yourself and which will take over any kind of a pattern that you submit to it and make that pattern permanent?

It's also an interesting thing that you can break any habit that you choose, and man is the only creature upon the face of this earth that can do that. Every animal below the level of man has its pattern fixed for it through what we call "instinct" and cannot go one step beyond that pattern that's been fixed for it by nature. You can choose any pattern you desire by which to guide your life and you can change that pattern as often as you choose. It would be extremely unfortunate if a man couldn't change his habits. If you had to take what nature sent you and couldn't modify that and change it, it'd be extremely unfortunate—there would be no use for a Science of Personal Achievement course. As a matter of fact, there couldn't be such a thing; it would be valueless unless you could use it for the purpose of converting your life as you desired, based upon habits voluntarily established.

Now let's see some of the habits that are fixed by cosmic habit force. First of all, the stars and planets are established in their fixed course. Isn't it an astounding thing to recognize that the astronomers can foretell the exact relationship of given planets and stars one hundred or two hundred years in advance? They couldn't do that unless there was a fixed pattern for the operation of this universe. We know there is. Man can fix his own pattern. He can make it anything he chooses. Most people, not understanding the law of cosmic habit force, not having the benefit of guidance of this philosophy, fix their habits based upon what? On ill health, misery, unhappiness, fear, failure, poverty, and all of the things that people don't want. Just as sure as you are here in this room, the predominating thoughts that you bring into your mind from day-to-day form the habits that will guide your life.

The subconscious mind doesn't know the difference between a penny and a million dollars, it doesn't know the difference between success and failure, and it doesn't care because the individual has already been given when he came over to this side everything that he needs with which to control his earthly destiny. He can't control what happened before he came over, he can't control what happens after he leaves here, but he certainly has the predominating right of influence over his entire destiny while he's on this planet. That's an astounding thing to recognize. A man doesn't control his destiny on this planet by accident or by haphazard procedures. He does it by having definite plans, then he repeats those plans over and over in his own mind until they are picked up by the subconscious mind, and then the subconscious mind undoubtedly is under the influence of cosmic habit force.

In the seasons of the year, as they come and go with regularity, and in the reproduction and growth of everything that grows from the soil of the earth, each seed reproducing precisely its own kind without variation, and the reproduction of every living thing, from the smallest insect and the microscopic protozoa that come up from the sea on up to man, everything, even the particles of matter, respond to habit as can be established by the law of chemistry. Everything is under this law of cosmic habit force.

If a student doesn't understand that he can set up his own habits and that there is a law that will help him carry it out—if he isn't taught that, if he doesn't get that basic truth, he hasn't been given a good foundation on which to build and use this philosophy. He must understand it. This subject of cosmic habit force is not one that the evangelist could use. There's not a lot of poetry in it. There's not a lot of opportunity to develop emotion in it. It's something that you have to deal with entirely through the processes of cold, calculating thought. It doesn't work you into a state of ecstasy. It does require some self-discipline for you to understand it, and a whole lot more self-discipline for you to apply it, but once you get a good grasp of it, it will give life and vitality and meaningfulness to all the other sixteen principles—every one of them. It wouldn't avail you anything at all if you just read this philosophy and said, "I agree with it," but didn't do anything about it—if you didn't start building a pattern for yourself based upon these seventeen principles. You know that that pattern is going to be picked up by the law of cosmic habit force in the exact proportion and extent that you are enthusiastic over it and that you have faith in connection with it.

Along with the profound gift of the Creator and the gift of the right of choice and complete control over the mind, the Creator has provided the means by which one may take full benefit of this gift. It consists of the law of cosmic habit force by which any self-made habit will be taken over and made into fixations which operate automatically.

Here are the conditions necessary to make use of the law of cosmic habit force. There are one, two, three.

One, there must be a purpose and a plan for its fulfillment worked out by the individual. The law of cosmic habit force is not going to benefit you unless you give it guidance and direction. You give it guidance and direction by laying out a plan of what it is you want to accomplish, writing it down, and submitting it to your subconscious mind through continuous repetition.

Second, the plan must be properly timed according to the nature and extent of the purpose. While I was out in Detroit recently, a former student or fan of mine called me on the telephone. He said, "Mister Hill, I am very much disappointed in your philosophy."

I said, "Yes? Give me the details."

He said, "I got *Think and Grow Rich* six months ago. I read it two or three times. I laid out a definite plan like you said—I put it on paper—and it doesn't work, and I'm losing confidence in it."

I said, "What was the plan? Read it to me."

He said, "My plan was to have one million dollars within one year."

I said, "Yes, but what did you intend to give for the million dollars?"

"Well," he said, "everything I have."

I said, "Well, it wasn't enough."

It wasn't enough. See, he had an entirely wrong concept of the philosophy. We don't run into people like that often, but now and then you will find one who expects that all he's got to do is to read this philosophy and presto, the wand of success will be put into his hands. He doesn't have a plan. It doesn't work that way. Why do you suppose the Creator gave man control—complete control—over but one thing and that is the power to use his own mind? Don't you suspect the Creator intended for that prerogative to be used? He certainly didn't give it to you to fritter away in idleness. He didn't mean for it to atrophy and die through disuse; he wanted you to use that. Because the Creator did give you control over but one thing, he must have had in mind that this one thing would be all that you need, and it is. If you take possession of your own mind and direct it to ends of your own choice systematically according to this philosophy, you're bound to make your life exactly what you want it to be.

Next, there must be constant repetition of the purpose. That's why I have my invisible guides. I can't go around from day to day devoting all my time to telling my subconscious mind what I want it to do; I've got a set of invisible guides that do that for me. There must be constant repetition of the purpose, under highly established emotionalized conditions such as faith and enthusiasm, until the pattern of the purpose is clearly fixed in the subconscious mind.

While on that subject of enthusiasm, I couldn't say too much to warn you against the danger of letting your enthusiasm run away with you. It's just as dangerous to have overenthusiasm as it is to have under enthusiasm, and if I had to choose between the two, I'd take the under enthusiasm. Enthusiasm is a dangerous thing. The very moment you go into a state of ecstasy, anybody who understands the operation of the mind finds that the windows and the doors of your mind are wide open, and he can walk right in on you.

I had that demonstrated very forcefully a good many years ago when I was conducting a school of advertising and salesmanship at the Bryant and Stratton College in Chicago. My friend Elbert Hubbard had just gone down on the ship Lusitania and been drowned, and immediately, his public relations people got busy and started advertising his series of books called *Little Journeys*. I was on his mailing list, of course, and they sent me a letter saying that they would be delighted to send me a photograph of the late Elbert Hubbard with his autograph on it if I would send in for it. Well, I sent in for it, and in just a little while, two high-powered salesmen came in to deliver the autographed photograph. One of them was a high-powered salesman, and the other was a trainee. He was training the other fellow how to do it. They said they had come to deliver the photograph, and boy, I was in a state of ecstasy. I started selling the Elbert Hubbard photographs like nobody's business, and when I got through, this training man said, "Well, Mister Hill, we knew that you'd not only want the photograph, but you would also want your friend's set of *Little Journeys,* and here's the order, it costs so much." And then I let out a horse laugh.

I said, "Well, I have been teaching my people not to be swayed too much with enthusiasm, and here I fall into my own trap."

By that time, this master salesman said to the trainee, "Let's get out of here." In other words, I was just ruining his trainee, don't you know. I had overexposed myself by being too enthusiastic, by doing too much talking instead of listening.

I heard a man say quite recently, "There are four holes in the head through which you can get knowledge and only one through which you can get it out, so you'd better be careful about how you use the one through which you get it out." It's not a bad idea to keep in mind, is it? Talking too much. You know, in selling, most salesman make the bad mistake of trying to do all the talking. The finest thing that a salesman can do is to ask questions and get his prospect to start talking. I don't know anything that equals it. In the first place, you cater to the ego of the prospective buyer, but more important than that, you're finding out exactly how his mind's working. And if it's not working along the lines that you want, you can turn the record over and play the other side, change your tempo, just as I do, for instance, when I'm lecturing. If I sense a single negative mind in an audience of a thousand, I can tell almost where it is, and I change my tempo immediately. And if I'm selling, I do the same thing. There's no use of going along and boring people with a talk when you know very well they're not getting it. You're just wasting your time until you know that you're in harmony with the person who is listening to you.

The most complex, mysterious, hard to understand reality of life is the human mind, how it operates and the things that can be accomplished with it by the individual himself. Generally speaking, one of the strange things that I found as I began to analyze these men of great achievement is that there's very, very little connection between schooling and success. I never in all my life, in all of my dealings with these outstanding men, found one that hadn't succeeded in almost exact ratio to the extent that he had failed somewhere along the line, oftentimes many times. Failure, defeat, adversity, and heartbreak can be a great blessing. When a man learns to take his adversities, his defeats, and his unpleasant circumstances and weave them into something useful, then he's on the high road to success, believe you me, because in the very nature of things, the Creator has designed it so that no man can go through life without some defeats and without some unpleasantness and without some failures. It's planned. Nobody can bypass that. If a man could bypass it, can you imagine living with a man that had never been defeated, never had any failures, and never had any adversities? Could you imagine living with a—well, I won't call him—I almost told you what kind of a man he would be, but I won't do that. Just say this, you couldn't live with him.

And I'll tell you another thing: I find that the people who get the most out of this course the quickest are the ones who had a lot of defeat because they have come to recognize they don't have all of the answers; they need some help from the outside. I don't know, ladies and gentlemen, how to do anything for anybody who doesn't want something or doesn't need something. This philosophy will be of no value whatsoever to anybody who doesn't need something or who doesn't want anything. The man who already has everything he wants—you can do nothing for him.

I had a peculiar experience with a student in Chicago about ten years ago. He said, "Mister Hill, I have been trying to get my wife to come down here with me, and she not only won't come down here with me, but she also ridicules me for spending money that she wanted to spend for carpets. Now, how can I get her down here?"

I said, "I don't know your wife, but I do know women in general, and I'll tell you how I would do it. I'd take a copy of *Think and Grow Rich* home with me and I'd hide it under my coat, and when she seemed to be not looking, but I'd make sure she was looking, I'd put it in some drawer that could be locked, and I'd turn the key and put the key in my pocket and get out just as fast as I could. When you come back from class each night, before you go to bed, you go there and sneak that book out under your coat and go into the bathroom and read it awhile then come back and sneak it in there."

"Well," he said, "what's that for?"

I said, "You'll find out what that's for."

The third night, when he came home the third time, she'd broken open the drawer and was reading the book in bed and said, "Why in the world didn't you tell me what was in this book before?"

He said, "I tried to but you wouldn't listen".

I don't know whether you're trout fishermen or not. I used to be. And I used to think it would be nice if I tossed the bait right in front of where I knew there's a trout hiding under a log. I soon found out that was not what the trout wanted at all. He wanted to let you know he was smart enough to find the food without your bringing it to him, because there's all this suspicion in the back of his mind that there was a hook in whatever you were handing him. And people are really like that. Things that you try to push on to people too fast—they wonder what's wrong with them. Isn't that right? Hasn't that been your experience? If you want to make a man easy to catch, make it hard for him to get what you have.

When I was running the school of advertising and sales-manship in Bryant and Stratton College, a young doctor came out from Oklahoma City and wanted to enroll in my school. He said, "Doctor Hill, I am a young doctor. I just completed a medical training course. But I have decided I want to go into the advertising business, and I've come over here to take your course provided that you can sell me." He said, "I know that you are an expert salesman. Now start in. I'm ready. Start in."

What do you suppose I did? I said, "I'm sure that you don't know the rules under which we operate. We don't take anybody into this school until they have proved to us conclusively that advertising is the field they should get into." That floored him. That really floored him. I said, "Instead of my starting in to sell you, you start in to sell me because you have to have spent at least four years in college and several thousand dollars learning medicine, and I'm not going to advise you to ditch that and to jump into advertising unless you give me a mighty good reason why you should get into this course."

Well, if you ever saw a miracle happen—he started in talking. He talked for half an hour, and when he got through, he said, "Doctor Hill, I like your story, I like your sales talk, and get me the blank, I'm ready to sign up." He sold himself. I hadn't opened my mouth. Is that something? It's a good thing to let the other fellow talk. Don't do all the talking yourself. Let the other fellow talk because every time you open your mouth, you reflect what's going on in your mind to whoever happens to be near you. Just remember that.

An experienced speaker, an experienced lawyer, or an experienced preacher can tell when he's looking into the faces of his audience or of a person to whom he's talking whether his talks are going over or not. If a man is buying what you're saying, he expresses it in his face, in his eyes, in the movements of his hands. When a man sits back with his lips tightly closed and his arms folded like that, looking like a wooden Indian while you're giving your sales talk, you just know that you're not getting across. But when he loosens up and begins to do this, then you know you're getting across. I can tell right now that you've had about all of me that you want this morning, and I'm going to close. Thank you very much. Thank you.

Narrator: *We know that you are excited and inspired by your Science of Personal Achievement program, and we suggest that if you have not already done so, that you sit down right now and write out your definite major purpose in life, for without a definite purpose, setting goals alone will have little meaning. This should consist of whatever it is in life you've always wanted to do. It is* *important that this be a written statement and that you read it aloud with great enthusiasm every morning and every evening. Don't be alarmed if you don't think of one immediately. Simply give your subconscious mind a command to provide you with a definite major purpose by a specific day and time, then relax and let it happen. Remember, if you have an idea, a service, or a product that will benefit your fellow man, no matter how extraordinary it may sound to other people, you can and will achieve what you desire if you believe you can and persistently act on that belief.*

In closing, here is a special message from Dr. Napoleon Hill:

Dr. Hill: And now may I reach out across the space and the time which separates us and offer you a hand of friendship and a sincere prayer that you will be blessed with a richer and a fuller life because of this message. Your big opportunity may be right where you are now. Follow these instructions faithfully and it will reveal itself to you. This is Napoleon Hill saying, "Don't search for opportunity in the distance but recognize it and embrace it right where you are."

About the Author

Napoleon Hill is one of the most well-known self-help authors of all time. His book, *Think and Grow Rich*, has sold over 100 million copies since it was written in 1937.